LEEDS:
SHAPING THE CITY

RIBA ┊┼┼┊ **Publishing**

Leeds
CITY COUNCIL

© RIBA ENTERPRISES LTD AND LEEDS CITY COUNCIL, 2009

Published by RIBA Publishing, part of RIBA Enterprises Ltd
15 Bonhill Street
London EC2P 2EA

ISBN 978 1 85946 244 7
Stock Code 61864

Written by: Martin Wainwright
Photo Editor: Jerry Hardman-Jones
Jerry's archive can be found at www.jh-jphoto.co.uk
Publisher: Steven Cross
Project Editor: Susan George
Copy Editor: Ian McDonald
Designed by Kneath Associates
Printed and bound by Cambridge University Press

Photographs and illustrations have been supplied by www.jh-jphoto.co.uk.
Additional picture research was undertaken by Jerry Hardman-Jones with
the exception of some of the case study images in Chapter 2 which have
been supplied separately and are credited accordingly within the text.
Every effort has been made to contact copyright holders. Queries should
be addressed to RIBA Publishing, 15 Bonhill Street, London EC2P 2EA

RIBA Publishing is part of RIBA Enterprises Ltd.
www.ribaenterprises.com

Front cover photograph © Jerry Hardman-Jones www.jh-jphoto.co.uk

CONTENTS

LEEDS: SHAPING THE CITY

FOREWORD

SUNAND PRASAD
Royal Institute of British Architects, President 2007-2009

The redevelopment and regeneration of Leeds is strongly evident in the attitude of its people, in a return to self confident architecture, and in the re-emergence of a strong sense of place in the city centre. Seen by some outsiders as a sprawling 'factoryopolis', Leeds has done exceptionally well in developing itself into a modern, thriving city. From the brash confidence of the days of Arthur Ransome, Leeds has enthusiastically and successfully embraced big challenges and opportunities.

Leeds is rare amongst British cities in employing a Civic Architect. John Thorp fills the role with a caring passion, which has earned him national respect and recognition. John's adoption of the concept of 'urban dentistry' has been the guiding light behind the many changes that have happened in central Leeds over the last thirty years. The combination of contemporary, radical architecture interspersed with the existing historic buildings, and attention to urban space and place, have all led to a city evolving and developing, while never forgetting its past. This 'urban dentistry' is evident in projects such as the glass-fronted building at 15/16 Park Row, the colour-panelled Crown Street apartments opposite Brodrick's Corn Exchange, and the neat insertion of Harvey Nichol's shop front in Briggate.

Leeds has produced its own wealth of local architectural talent – most notably Benjamin Latrobe, who co-designed the Washington Capitol and the White House with Thomas Jefferson. And Cuthbert Brodrick who left an unparalleled mark on the city with the Town Hall, Corn Exchange and Mechanics' Institute (now the new City Museum).

But the city has also welcomed architects from outside its boundaries, Sir Terry Farrell has advised on the latest large-scale development between Vicar Lane and Mabgate; and the boldest of the new era of skyscrapers, are the work of Ian Simpson from Manchester and Ken Shuttleworth, who was responsible for the Swiss Re building in London during his time at Lord Norman Foster's partnership.

The transformation of Leeds is evident for all who visit today, and the physical expression of Leeds' success – seen everywhere from the trendy clubs and restaurants to the cool city-centre loft apartments – keeps energising new generations of people.

There remain considerable challenges, above all tackling climate change through town planning and architecture. There are also great opportunities ahead that Leeds will doubtless rise to. It has shown how to use design to create an urban fabric of quality and comfort for the people who live and work there, and for those who are simply passing through.

< Symbol of Leeds
WWW.JH-JPHOTO.CO.UK

PREFACE

COUNCILLOR RICHARD BRETT
COUNCILLOR ANDREW CARTER
Joint Leaders of Leeds City Council

We are immensely fortunate in Leeds to have many excellent historic buildings, and an architectural heritage that is world class. We have not destroyed the past, but have adapted buildings to meet new needs, have refurbished and extended in a way which is sympathetic to the unique place that Leeds is, with spaces and buildings that are for people.

In recent years we have seen the pace of development increase dramatically, and this has given us the opportunity to reinvent the city. Our new developments have enhanced our city, creating an urban fabric that is of high quality and which feels comfortable to live in. Our concerns for design have been as much about the space between buildings as for the buildings themselves. We haven't got everything right all of the time, but we have ensured that Leeds has remained a big city which is human in its feel and scale. Through the Leeds Renaissance Framework we have established a set of guiding principles that will shape the future development of the city. This book is structured around these principles.

At the end of 2007 when much of this book was written, there was over £7 bn of major new developments either proposed or with planning permission. A small amount of this development is currently on hold because of the 'credit crunch', however, Leeds is well placed to come out of the economic downturn stronger than ever.

We are proud of our great city and we are proud of our partnership working. This book is an excellent example of the latter, and a superb advert for the former. It will help us all understand our city and will help us shape the future.

In Leeds, private and public sectors work hand in hand and this book is also testament to that. We are grateful to our editorial team, to the RIBA, to our photographer and editor who are all clearly passionate about Leeds.

Finally, to you the reader, to our architects, developers and businesses. Let us work together to achieve the highest standards of design, to ensure Leeds remains a place that we can all be proud of.

< Leeds Town Hall and Millennium Square Fountain
WWW.JH-JPHOTO.CO.UK

RICHARD MORAN / WWW.MORANPHOTO.CO.UK

ACKNOWLEDGEMENTS

I would like to thank my fellow members of the editorial team for long, cheerful and careful discussions which have brought this book into being.

They are Elizabeth Minkin, an honorary fellow of the RIBA, who played an important role in Leeds' development as a senior councillor, until her retirement in May; John Thorp MBE, Britain's only Civic Architect, of whom much more shortly; Paul Stephens, Leeds City Council's Chief Economic Services Officer; Peter Vaughan, major projects officer in the City Council's development department; and Jerry Hardman-Jones, whose photographs are worth more than many thousand words. Professor Neil Jackson was also invaluable to the team and contributed the thoughtful introductions to the five sections of Chapter Two before moving from Leeds to the architectural department of Liverpool University. We have all been helped enormously by Steven Cross of RIBA Publishing who oversaw the project and his colleague Susan George whose work on seeing it to publication has been invaluable. Many thanks also to successive leaders of Leeds' City Council Andrew Carter, Mark Harris and Richard Brett, to the city's Director of Development Jean Dent and to Brenda Carter of the Development Directorate Support Team.

Martin Wainwright

< Civic Hall and Millennium Square Ice Rink
WWW.JH-JPHOTO.CO.UK

^ Red brick; Leeds' basic material
WWW.JH-JPHOTO.CO.UK

PUBLISHING PARTNERS

We would like to thank all of the companies and organisations listed here who have generously supported the publication of this wonderful book.

The development and regeneration of Leeds is a success story for all those involved – from those working within the City Council, the investors, developers, architects and contractors who have supported and backed the redevelopment plans, to, ultimately, the local businesses, people and communities.

None of what you will see and read in this book could have been achieved without the support and encouragement of companies and organisations like those listed. We thank them for their support and look forward to working with them in the future.

Sunand Prasad
Councillor Richard Brett
Councillor Andrew Carter

careyjones

MEPC

Renaissance Leeds

< River Aire by the Royal Armouries
WWW.JH-JPHOTO.CO.UK

careyjones

CAREYJONES

For over 20 years careyjones has enjoyed an enviable reputation for award-winning design across all sectors; specialising in architecture, masterplanning and interior design. Founded in Leeds in 1987 by Gordon Carey and Chris Jones, careyjones has transformed over the intervening years into an internationally known Practice which now operates out of four design studios in London, Leeds, Manchester and New York.

The Practice has always been committed to helping Leeds become a world class city having being involved in many landmark and regeneration developments over the years including; Princes Exchange, Whitehall Waterfront, Clarence Dock and Wellington Place, plus a number of high profile projects for the University of Leeds. careyjones prides itself on maintaining strong links with the local community and remains closely involved and committed to organisations such as St Georges Crypt as well as helping to establish the North's first Breast Cancer Haven at The Gateway.

careyjones is committed to sustainable design and business practices.

EVANS
property group

EVANS PROPERTY GROUP

The Evans Property Group is one of the largest privately owned group of companies in the north of England. The group has been active in the property market in Leeds for over 70 years. It currently has over £250m invested in the City.

The group specialises in major regeneration projects and owns considerable tracts of land within the City. It is working with the relevant public authorities and communities to bring about large scale redevelopment and sustainable regeneration in various areas of the City.

Evans Easyspace is one of the groups associated companies providing flexible accommodation mainly to small and medium sized companies. It has over 60 business centres nationwide and provides accommodation for over 1,500 businesses. Approximately 7,000 people are employed in the Centres.

^ River Aire, Millennium Bridge, redeveloped warehouses and docks
WWW.JH-JPHOTO.CO.UK

GLEEDS

Gleeds has over 120 years experience in the property and construction industry and currently employs over 1,500 people in 48 offices across five continents – making us one of the world's leading management and construction consultants.

With the background, resources and financial strength to undertake complex, multi-national contracts, Gleeds has a global reach and the wealth of experience to cover every client requirement. Our wide experience in virtually every sector means that our clients benefit from an extensive international office network, providing local knowledge and highly skilled and flexible professionals.

Our vision is to create a business that attracts the very best clients, projects and people in the industry.

HAMMERSON PLC

Hammerson plc is a FTSE-100 Real Estate Investment Trust which operates principally in the retail sector in the UK and France. Its £7 billion portfolio, which provides 1.3 million m² of retail space and 280,000 m² of offices, includes 14 major shopping centres and 19 retail parks.

Hammerson has a track record of successfully carrying out major city centre regeneration projects. Recent award-winning developments include Bishops Square in London and Bullring in Birmingham. In September 2008 the Company opens three major retail-led developments: Highcross, Leicester; Cabot Circus, Bristol and an extension to Parinor, an existing centre in Paris.

The Company is currently working with several councils to deliver retail-led mixed-use regeneration projects in cities including Aberdeen, Leeds and Sheffield.

For more information, visit www.hammerson.com.

^ The old Central Station site
WWW.JH-JPHOTO.CO.UK

MEPC

MEPC manages some of the UK's best known commercial property. With a £1.1bn portfolio, we are leader in our field. We have eight Business Estates in prime locations throughout the UK. Together they provide over 10m sq ft of high-quality space for more than 1,000 organisations, employing 20,000 people.

Our customers range from small start-ups and fast-growing businesses to successful multi-nationals across all industry sectors. They include science, media and telecoms companies, firms of lawyers and accountants and creative agencies.

Our Business Estates are all located in or near to large regional centres, providing customers with the benefits of excellent local and national transport links and access to skilled local workforces and infrastructure. Secure, landscaped grounds and convenient amenities and facilities make them ideal environments for people too.

For more information on MEPC visit www.mepc.com

QUARMBY | CONSTRUCTION

QUARMBY CONSTRUCTION CO LTD

Quarmby Construction Company is one of the largest privately owned construction companies in the North of England by turnover and experience with a diverse portfolio of high-value project commissions nationally.

From its offices in Ilkley near Leeds, the Company initiated and has played a prominent role in shaping Leeds City Centre for the 21st century, working with private partners and public authorities to deliver high-profile new and regeneration projects.

From the earliest renaissance of the City Centre waterfront to multiple, award-winning regeneration and new build schemes at Holbeck Urban Village, Wellington Place, Leeds Town Hall and The Electric Press, Millennium Square, Quarmby Construction continues to make a positive contribution to the built environment of the City of Leeds.

For more information visit www.quarmby.co.uk

Renaissance Leeds

RENAISSANCE LEEDS

The Renaissance Leeds Partnership is a collaboration between Leeds City Council, Yorkshire Forward, English Partnerships and the Leeds Initiative.

The key objective of the Partnership is to maximise public and private sector confidence and investment in the regeneration of Leeds. Its focus is on 'city shaping' and the definition and deep understanding of potential connections within the physical environment contributing to the delivery of the Vision for Leeds 2020.

The Renaissance Leeds Project provides a framework for partner organisations and investors to work within, guiding major physical investments in the city.
It helps to give clarity to where the city is going.

For more information visit www.leedsrisingcity.org

TIMELINE

^ Panorama, 1720
LEEDS LIBRARY AND INFORMATION SERVICE

731	Bede's History of the English Church and People mentions Leeds Parish Church, calling the settlement Loidis.	**1812**	Matthew Murray's steam engines begin operating on Middleton Railway.
1086	Leeds mentioned in the Domesday Book.	**1816**	Leeds–Liverpool canal is completed. Armley Park built for Benjamin Gott to designs by Robert Smirke.
1152	Foundations of Kirkstall Abbey laid.		
1155	Knights Templar establish base at Newsam, later Temple Newsam.	**1819**	The city is lit by gas in place of oil lamps.
		1822	Joshua Tetley founds his subsequently famous brewery.
1170	St John's Church, Adel, built; now the oldest surviving in Leeds.	**1831**	Leeds School of Medicine founded.
1207	Nobleman Maurice Paynel grants Leeds a charter.	**1832**	Cholera epidemic strikes in Leeds, killing 700. East Street Mills built to designs by John Clark.
1258	Market operating in Leeds.		
1469	Woollen industry well established in Leeds.	**1834**	Meanwood Hall built, designed by John Clark.
1552	Leeds Grammar School founded by Sir William Sheafield.	**1835**	Municipal Reform Act leads to election on limited franchise of first local council.
1560	First known sketch plan of Leeds, now in Public Record Office.	**1838–40**	John Marshall, flax-spinner and Liberal MP, builds Egyptian-style Temple Mill.
1626	King Charles I grants charter to Leeds, including 13 satellite villages covering 21,000 acres. Pre-eminent nationally as a cloth entrepôt, the town adopts a fleece on its coat of arms.	**1841**	New Parish Church opens, designed by Robert Chantrell.
		1842	Roundhay Hall built, designed by Samuel Sharpe.
		1847	Leeds prison at Armley built, designed by Perkin & Backhouse.
1628	Red Hall in the Headrow built, probably the first large house to be made from red brick, which later became Leeds' signature material.	**1848**	Mill Hill Unitarian chapel in City Square opens, designed by Bowman & Crowther.
1634	St John's Church, Briggate consecrated.	**1849**	Deadly cholera epidemic strikes, killing 2,000 and promoting major public health reform and construction of sewers.
1643	Civil War Battle of Leeds; Parliamentarians drive out Royalists.		
1645	Bubonic plague kills 1325.	**1858**	Leeds Town Hall opened by Queen Victoria, after Cuthbert Brodrick wins design competition and council votes after bitter debate to include his tower.
1662	Second charter from Charles II gives Leeds a mayor.		
1698	Celia Fiennes visits Leeds and finds it wealthy, large and clean.		
1715	Ralph Thoresby publishes the first history of Leeds 'Ducatus Leodiensis'.	**1859**	Thoresby Society founded to promote local history.
1718	Town's first newspaper the *Leeds Mercury* published; now part of the *Yorkshire Post*.	**1863**	The Corn Exchange opened, a masterpiece of engineering by Brodrick.
		1864	Only public execution ever held at Armley Jail. Thomas Harding opens Tower Works with three Italianate chimney towers which remain a favourite Leeds landmark.
1724	Daniel Defoe describes Briggate cloth market as 'A prodigy of its kind unequalled in the world'.		
1725	First detailed map of Leeds published by John Cossins.		
1745	Mob attacks John Wesley in the town.	**1864–9**	General Infirmary built to designs by Sir George Gilbert Scott.
1752	Kirkstall Grange built to designs by James Paine.	**1872**	Roundhay Park is bought by the city to furious accusations of wasting public funds.
1755	Street lighting introduced.		
1758	Middleton Colliery Railway opens, the world's first although only for goods, not passengers.	**1874**	Yorkshire College of Science founded, later to become Leeds University.
		1878	Thornton's Arcade and the Grand Theatre designed by George Corson opened. St Paul's House, designed in Moorish style by Thomas Ambler for ready-made clothing magnate Sir John Barran completed.
1765	First Leeds Infirmary opened in Kirkgate.		
1770	Leeds–Liverpool Canal commenced.		
1786	Denison Hall built to designs by William Lindley.		
1792	Benjamin Gott builds Bean Ing Mills, the first titan of the Industrial Revolution, on site now occupied by *Yorkshire Post*.	**1884**	Michael Marks launches his Penny Bazaar in Leeds Market, joining in 1894 with Thomas Spencer to found the famous department store.
1801	First census establishes population as just above 50,000.		
1808	Leeds Library completed in Commercial Street, designed by Thomas Johnson and with Joseph Priestley on the committee.	**1884**	Municipal Buildings designed by George Corson opened to house various Civic departments, Police and Central Library.

^ City motorway
WWW.JH-JPHOTO.CO.UK

1886	Whitelock's first city luncheon bar, now Leeds' most famous pub, opened to designs by Thomas Ambler.
1888	City Art Gallery opened to designs by W. H. Thorp, also architect of Leeds Medical School in 1894.
1890	Leeds Cricket, Football & Athletic Co founded at Headingley.
1893	Leeds becomes a city by Royal Charter.
1894	Electric tramways are started.
1899	Metropole Hotel built to designs by Chorley, Connon & Chorley.
1901	Population 178,000.
1903	The Black Prince and associated statues in City Square by Thomas Brock, Alfred Drury, H. C. Fehr and W. F. Pomeroy are unveiled, in a layout designed by William Bakewell.
1904	St Anne's Catholic Cathedral, designed by John Henry Eastwood and Sydney Kyffin Greenslade, consecrated. The County Arcade and other arcades, now united as the Victoria Quarter, are opened to designs by the celebrated 'theatre architect' Frank Matcham.
	University of Leeds granted its own Charter as an independent institution by King Edward VII. Oriental-style City Markets opened to designs by J. & J. Leeming.
1905	The first cinema in Leeds opened.
1911	Population 450,000.
1916	Frank Brangwyn's mosaics installed at St Aidan's, Harehills.
1919	Leeds United Football Club founded.
1922	First BBC broadcast from Leeds. Montague Burton's in Burmantofts becomes the largest clothing factory in the world.
1926	Wallace Arnolds launches first coach trip.
1928	Britain's first permanent traffic lights installed in Park Row.
1931	Headrow laid out to designs of Sir Reginald Blomfield.
1933	Leeds Civic Hall, designed by E. Vincent Harris, opened by King George V and Queen Mary.
1936	Leeds University's Parkinson Building begun to designs by Lancaster, Lucas & Lodge.
1938	Railway station opens, designed by W. H. Hamlyn, behind Queen's Hotel, designed by the same architect and W.Curtis Green.
1941	Worst air raid on Leeds – 60 killed. Quarry Hill flats opened to designs by city architect, R. A. H. Livett.
1959	Last tram in Leeds withdrawn from service.
1963	Launch of Leeds International Piano Competition.
1964	Merrion Centre opened as Leeds' first mall, designed by Gillinson, Barnett & Partners.
1971	Launch of city centre Pedestrian Precinct.
1974	Leeds becomes a Metropolitan District, embracing surrounding

	areas and increasing its population by half to 717,000.
1981	Riots in Chapeltown.
1988	Leeds Urban Development Corporation set up, lasting until 1995.
1989	Pedestrian Precinct redesigned as Landmark Leeds.
1990	West Yorkshire Playhouse opens, designed by the Appleton Partnership. Leeds Initiative established.
1992	Leeds Polytechnic becomes Leeds Metropolitan University.
1994	Leeds Architecture and Design Initiative (LADI) formed.
1995	Riverside regeneration gets under way.
	Royal Armouries Museum opens, designed by Derek Walker Associates and Lars Henning.
1996	Leeds hosts Euro 96 football matches.
1997	Harvey Nichols opens, designed by Brooker Flyn and catapulting Leeds on to the national retail map. Thackray Medical Museum opens at former Leeds Workhouse.
1998	No 1 City Square opens to designs by Abbey Hanson Rowe.
1999	Vision for Leeds published.
2000	Millennium Square opens, designed by John Thorp, Civic Architect.
2001	Nelson Mandela becomes honorary citizen. Census sets population at 715,404 (369,570 women and 345,834 men), making city the UK's third largest after London and Birmingham. Annual 4x4 planning and architecture seminars launched by architect Ian Tod.
2002	City Square remodelled by Civic Architect John Thorp.
2003	Launch of Leeds Property Forum.
2006	Grand Theatre reopens after year-long £23 million first phase of renovation.
2007	Output of Leeds' financial sector tops £13.5 billion. Bridgewater Place completed as the city's highest building, with 32 storeys designed by Aedas Architects.
2008	Leeds City Museum re-opens in the former Leeds Mechanics Institute on Millennium Square.

01
DRIVING CHANGE

You and I share a very good thing in common. We had
the luck to be born in Leeds. Now, for all kinds of reasons,
Leeds is one of the best places in the world in which to be
born. Let me tell you a few of them ...

Arthur Ransome writing in the June 1937 issue of
The Chimney Corner, Leeds public libraries' quarterly
magazine for children.

∧ City Square
WWW.JH-JPHOTO.CO.UK

∧ Riverside apartments
WWW.JH-JPHOTO.CO.UK

∧∧ Old 'Factory Leeds'

It was good in Arthur Ransome's day, it is hard to find an adjective that describes its fizz and chutzpah in the first decade of the 21st century. The city has been so successful in the last 30 years that its rivals have had to fall back on the insult 'smug', a jibe which, by definition, has little effect on its target. There is a deep-rooted sense of satisfaction, every bit as cosy as Ransome's, in the unofficial capital of Yorkshire. It shows mostly in the attitude of its people but also finds expression in the architecture, and especially in the strong sense of place in the city centre.

This may be self-satisfaction but it has an infectious feeling of comfort and content. Leeds has done exceptionally well in transforming itself from a grimy 'factoryopolis', and its people know that. There are

challenges ahead and an articulate group of critics, who are far from smug and who worry that the cutting edge might become less sharp. But the physical expression of Leeds' success – seen everywhere from clubs and cool restaurants to lofts above the inland port, where canal and river entwine – keep stimulating the imagination of new generations of entrepreneurs.

This fits into the tradition of a city which has grown through the centuries in a series of convulsions, each more energetic than the last and all leaving traces which have thankfully been preserved today. Little Woodhouse offers a delightful hillside of Georgian houses, stone-setted streets and (in contrast to the overwhelmingly residential landscape of a Bath or a Cheltenham)

∧ Victorian Railway Viaduct cut through parish church graveyard
WWW.JH-JPHOTO.CO.UK

curious, small industrial buildings from the 18th century, many of them smartly converted into house extensions, offices or workshops. On the other side of the city centre, the delicate relics of the White Cloth Hall and Assembly Rooms, inevitably transformed into smart eating places, are attractive in themselves but more interesting as survivors from the days of Leeds' ruthless Victorian city fathers.

For Leeds is self-evidently not a place which has preserved its architectural history in aspic. It nods politely to the past but does not doff its cap. In 1969, the Poet Laureate John Betjeman wrote the preface to *The Historic Architecture of Leeds* by Derek Linstrum, and was rather schoolmasterly: 'The individuality of Leeds is expressed in its buildings, private mansions, public halls and churches – if Leeds loses these buildings it might just as well be a bit of that international nothingness that is turning so many of our historic and industrial cities into cheap imitations of America.' This assessment still applies up to a point, but only so far. A better definition of Leeds' character is to be found in the way that the city has combined a sense of tradition with a restless energy for change.

From the windows of the lavatories in Pizza Express at the White Cloth Hall, you look straight into the carriages of trains from York and the Northeast waiting for the signals to let them into Leeds City Station. The railway was smashed like an axe across the diagonal of the Cloth Hall's colonnaded square. Halifax's Piece Hall is a grander version of what was largely lost here. A few yards further on, the ancestors of the 19th-century developers repose at a steep angle in graves that the railway relaid on its embankments after shoving the parish church cemetery aside.

The process recurred when Alderman William Lupton steered the Headrow through Leeds' planning committees in 1924, sweeping away mucky side streets to give his city a single east–west boulevard of almost Parisian grandeur. Baron Haussmann's hidden agenda of providing a clear field of fire for government troops in order to cow the French capital would certainly apply here. More cheerfully, the Headrow's rise and fall, on slopes created artificially by the alderman's team, has regularly been suggested as ideal for a San Francisco-style cable car, running between Westgate and Eastgate. Like the central line of trees and shrubs which led to

< Aerial photo of Headrow, Leeds in 1939
LEEDS LIBRARY AND INFORMATION SERVICES

17

∧ Eastgate Fountain
WWW.JH-JPHOTO.CO.UK

∧ Gotts Park Mansion, Armley
WWW.JH-JPHOTO.CO.UK

the Headrow being nicknamed the 'Hedgerow' when they were planted in the late 1960s, such a move would add some light relief to its parallel lines of monumental buildings, which were mostly the work of the London architect Sir Reginald Blomfield. Whether such a proposal will ever be realised, however, remains to be seen.

In both great developments, the railway and the Headrow, there were some losses for Leeds but much greater gains. And Blomfield's work, which includes an eye-catching rotunda at the eastern end of the new road – initially the country's most inaccessible petrol station run by the long-standing Leeds garage chain Appleyard's, and now the Eastgate Fountain – is typical of another force that has shaped Leeds. Blomfield was one of a distinguished line of nationally rated architects to be invited to the city from elsewhere. Sir Robert Smirke designed Gott's Park Mansion in 1820, above its Humphry Repton park in what is now inner-city Armley. Sir George Gilbert Scott completed the Leeds General Infirmary in 1868. Nugent Cachemaille-Day built the striking, and now Grade I-listed, Church of the Epiphany in 1938 on the Gipton housing estate. In 1960, the Modernists Sir John Burnet, Tait and Partners were responsible for Benton Park comprehensive school at Rawdon.

Notwithstanding this, Leeds has produced its own wealth of local architectural talent – most notably Benjamin Latrobe, who co-designed the Washington Capitol

and the White House with Thomas Jefferson but alas built nothing in his home town, where he was born in 1764, the son of the headmaster of Fulneck school and supervisor of all Moravian schools in Britain. Cuthbert Brodrick, who did stay at home, left an unparalleled mark on Leeds with the Town Hall, Corn Exchange and Mechanics' Institute – the last now the new City Museum. But the city has never burdened itself with a parochial hostility to outsiders. Sir Terry Farrell is advising on the latest large-scale development between Vicar Lane and Mabgate; and the boldest of the many skyscrapers, which are the next planned change to the Leeds skyline, are the work of Ian Simpson from Manchester and Ken Shuttleworth, who was responsible for the London 'Gherkin' (Swiss Re building) during his time at Lord Norman Foster's partnership. Even when the Royal Fine Arts Commission chaired by Norman St John Stevas insisted that London architects be involved in the new sculpture gallery at Leeds City Art Gallery on the Headrow in 1982, the chosen partnership of Casson Conder did not get a chilly welcome. The Civic Architect John Thorp did much of the work and there was a particular cause for quiet local satisfaction: an internal competition organised as an exercise in the planning department saw one bright spark come up with the notion of a glass pyramid for the gallery's entrance. It didn't happen, but Leeds can truthfully say that it anticipated the Louvre.

Today's city, however, is not all the work of careful planning and rational thought. Luck has played her

> Corn Exchange
LEEDS LIBRARY AND
INFORMATION SERVICES

> The Mechanics
Institute
LEEDS LIBRARY AND
INFORMATION SERVICES

< Leeds
Town Hall, 1928
LEEDS LIBRARY AND
INFORMATION SERVICES

∧ Leeds General Infirmary façade
LEEDS LIBRARY AND INFORMATION SERVICES

∧ The 'hidden' inner ring road under construction
ENGLISH HERITAGE/AEROFILMS ARCHIVE

∧ The 'hidden' inner ring road
WWW.JH-JPHOTO.CO.UK

∧∧ Quarry Hill flats 1951
ENGLISH HERITAGE/AEROFILMS ARCHIVE

part too. Unrestrained by outside events, the drive of the Victorians and the urban improvers of the 1920s and 30s could have swept too much away. In the civic archives there is a revealing, almost frightening, design from 1937 for a vast new museum on the Headrow, which would have tipped the road's scale from boulevard to *Brave New World*. In the same utopian spirit, after visiting Vienna's Karl Marx Hof, the then city housing director R. A. H. Livett built the Quarry Hill flats between 1934 and 1940. At the time this was by some way Europe's largest municipal housing complex, its vast grey concrete bow facing the Eastgate entry to the Headrow. It looked noble from the air – better still from a satellite – and incorporated a great many novelties, such as the Garchey suction refuse system, which were influential in later public housing. But only a handful of devotees mourned its demolition in 1976–8, which cleared the way for today's stimulating mixture of buildings on the grassy rise which the flats once encircled. In the Leeds spirit of saving aspects of every era's building, it might have been nice to have kept a fragment of Quarry Hill: perhaps one of the vast horseshoe gateways cut in the walls – said to have been admired by Hitler, who considered the place as a northern invasion headquarters. But the concrete was

sub-standard and the workmanship generally deemed too rickety to preserve, although that in itself might have been a useful object lesson.

Inevitably in the great rebuilding era after the Second World War, there was a renewed threat of 'leviathan planning' returning to Leeds, although the city had very few bombsites after an almost miraculous escape from Nazi blitzes. The bombers had had higher-priority targets and the complex, smoky valleys of West Yorkshire were hard to navigate from the air. A north–south motorway along the line of Albion Street was suggested in the 1960s but thankfully given short shrift on cost grounds. Although the then Conservative council headed by Frank, later Lord, Marshall briefly used the slogan 'Motorway City of the Seventies' on locally posted mail, the inner ring road remained east–west only, relatively modest and entirely buried in tunnels and cuttings. Leeds thus avoided the Grand Prix racetrack fate inflicted on parts of central Birmingham at the time. An elephantine project to rebuild the entire Leeds General Infirmary on an Olympian scale also remained a blueprint because of its equally enormous cost.

These 'escapes from vastness' have played a part in the architectural thinking which governs modern Leeds,

^ Tile from the Turkish Baths
WWW.JH-JPHOTO.CO.UK

^ Ladies Plunge Pool from the old demolished Turkish Baths
WWW.JH-JPHOTO.CO.UK

^ The office of Civic Architect, John Thorp
WWW.JH-JPHOTO.CO.UK

along with a recognition of the accumulated legacy of previous generations' buildings. The city is one of the last in Britain to employ a Civic Architect, and John Thorp fills the role with a thoughtfulness which has earned national respect. You may meet him picking up ginkgo leaves from the imaginative new plantings in the city centre, or salvaging tesserae from the long-demolished Turkish Baths on Cookridge Street to make rubbings which, like the leaves, he uses in his handmade Christmas cards. Or you may be lucky enough to be invited to his office (which, nomad-like, seems to be in a different nook of the many large civic buildings every year). Here, the walls are lined with vivid geometrical diagrams of 'How the City Works': intersecting circles show quarters and gateways; routes

and walkways curve into the petals of an enormous flower; the Inner Loop, terror of all first-time visitors in cars, wiggles like a demented snake.

Amongst it all, and against a wall of photographs and drawings of inspirational buildings from across the world, Thorp explains the concept of 'urban dentistry', which has gently guided the wholesale change in central Leeds over the last three decades. Initiated by the city council's planning department, it became the guiding principle of Leeds when the planners joined Thorp and other built-environment colleagues in an enlarged and more influential Development Department in 2003.

Filling, polishing, bridging – all the technical terms of the dentist apply to the approach which, like good dental

∨ Turkish Baths on
Cookridge Street
LEEDS LIBRARY AND
INFORMATION SERVICES

^ Boules Piste in Bond Court
WWW.JH-JPHOTO.CO.UK

ˇ Bridge End 'Flat Iron'
WWW.JH-JPHOTO.CO.UK

ˇ Princes Exchange
WWW.JH-JPHOTO.CO.UK

^ The Bourse reflects its
Victorian neighbours
WWW.JH-JPHOTO.CO.UK

ˇ Royal Amusements
WWW.JH-JPHOTO.CO.UK

work, starts by respecting what is already there. But that is only the prelude. The urban dentist then looks for improvement, new use and neglected spaces which might be 'greened' or provide a setting for public art – or even, as in the otherwise uniformly 1960/70s piazza of Bond Court, house a French boules piste in a grove of trees. He or she does not shrink either from more dramatic infilling, such as the mirrored curve of The Bourse in Boar Lane or the circular CASPAR flats by the inner ring road – the latter's experimental construction eventually proving its undoing, but not before valuable long-term lessons for low-cost social housing had been learned. The critics of 'smug' Leeds regularly mock the lack of a single iconic work of modern architectural splendour in the city centre. But Thorp and his colleagues respond that there are many modest icons – old, new and sometimes a conjunction of both – which together make up something just as distinctive as a Foster tower or a 'shard' designed by Renzo Piano or Daniel Libeskind.

This strategy has deep historical roots but it also developed from the more recent, late-20th-century development of Leeds. After the Second World War and a period of austerity and national recovery, the city had its share of new and, as it seemed at the time, bold buildings. Tower blocks mushroomed, including three

pairs of grandiose 'gateways' at Swarcliffe on the A64 York Road, as well as the westward M621 spur to the M62 and on the approach into Leeds from the south, which risked placing the needs of tenants second to making a civic statement. The Brutalist Yorkshire Post Building in Wellington Street dates from the same era, a move by the newspaper which lost the city the Post's fine Edwardian offices in Albion Street, replaced in 1970 by the unadorned block of West Riding House. The top floors of this form an excellent viewpoint, because you cannot see the block itself, and the Post Building is original enough to earn recognition in the longer run. But neither has made many friends yet. The same might be thought true of the Westgate 'Olympic' Swimming Pool, although this particular building inspired a surprisingly vigorous campaign against its demolition and a notable final bow as a sensational gallery for a temporary installation by the German artists, the Office for Subversive Architecture, in the empty pool. Even more Brutalist than the *Yorkshire Post* offices, Leeds International Pool, dating from 1967, is technically interesting and has been described as the only work of any value by the vast practice belonging to the corrupt Yorkshire architect John Poulson. The proposed replacement scheme for it is a striking design by Make architects.

This era also gave the city such large but little-loved blocks as City House beside the railway station and the mall, office towers and multi-storey car park of the Merrion Centre. The latter was Leeds' first modern attempt to match the wonderful Victorian arcades which have been an elegant and commercially successful defence against Yorkshire weather for more than a century. Although not distinguished architecturally, the centre is interesting as an example of planning on a large scale, with definite ambitions in the mind of its developer in 1965, the late Arnold Ziff. He deliberately introduced cutting-edge novelties such as travelators and commissioned artwork, showing notable modesty in the latter process. A sculpture competition judged by experts in the field, including Sir Herbert Read, was won by Glenn Hellman's *Androgyne*, an unpopular choice with shoppers and Ziff himself, but one which he respected because he had agreed the terms of the competition and felt bound to honour them. A set of original Rowland

donated to the centre where they whirred and whirled regularly in a glass stand which displayed them in turn, proved some compensation as everyone loved them. *Androgyne* now stands in a little-used concrete well, a corner of urban transgression in the booming heart of Leeds which has its own forlorn appeal.

There was one other spectacular development at this time, in the somewhat self-contained world of Leeds University. Here, a striking collection of stark concrete buildings surrounding Chancellor's Court are an iconic reminder of 1960s architectural style. But they too were not instantly loved, and the public's reaction against the decade of large grey and blocky landmarks played a part in Leeds' next period of development. Much more modest, it nonetheless seemed to be very highly planned, or perhaps excessively subject to local planning guidelines – so much so that its uniformity became teasingly known as the 'Leeds Look'. Red-brick façades, circular windows and scaled-down stone pediments were its hallmarks and they can be seen in many of the city's 1980s buildings. Most are unremarkable, but occasionally the Leeds Lookers went overboard. Those 'acquitted by the Bench' or found guilty of only minor offences must find it hard not to smile as they leave the fancy, purple, pink and green-painted confection of Leeds Magistrates Court. Architectural critics were never mollified, however. Ken Powell of the *Daily Telegraph* branded the Look as embodying 'the offence of the inoffensive' and a series of spirited debates organised by the Leeds Society of Architects and Leeds Civic Trust played a part in moving planning guidelines on.

And so the city stood towards the end of the 1980s, when something altogether more ambitious was set

 Leeds Magistrates Court
WWW.JH-JPHOTO.CO.UK

^ Leeds Waterfront
WWW.JH-JPHOTO.CO.UK

in train. In spite of all its changes and improvements, Leeds still suffered from an image down South of a grimy, gritty northern industrial town. There was enough tat and grubbiness in reality for this notion to be sustained even when people ventured up for a brief visit, although it was not remotely the true picture. And so a collection of determined institutions and individuals decided that this must change.

Reform was helped by the politics of the time. Mrs Thatcher's government was suspicious of big city councils (which her Conservative predecessors had greatly enlarged in the local government reforms of 1973–4), and it created urban development corporations to take over their planning powers in key areas. Leeds was one of them, to much local fury. The debate continues, still with a certain amount of passion, to this day. But whatever the political rights and wrongs, between 1988 and 1995 the Leeds Development Corporation (LDC) offered an alternative to the long-established monopoly of the council. It earned respect

from local planners by showing that contemporary, radical architecture could be a good neighbour to existing historic buildings, an example later followed at Number 15/16 Park Row, the colour-panelled Crown Street apartments opposite Brodrick's Corn Exchange, and the neat insertion of Harvey Nichols's shopfront on Briggate are 3 examples of successful contemporary style insertions approved after the demise of the Development Corporation. It used its extra money, simpler systems and freedom from all the responsibilities of public office to press ahead with crucial schemes. The beginning of the transformation of Leeds waterfront, a milestone in the city's modern architectural history, owed much to the LDC and is suitably commemorated by a water sculpture in the Calls called *Regeneration*. As its chairman, the supermarket entrepreneur Peter Hartley, said in his final report: 'It made things happen.'

Not always for the best, however: the LDC's attempts to regenerate the semi-suburban Kirkstall Valley

26

were clumsy and left a legacy of resentment at an overbearing commercial Big Brother chucking its weight about. Labour politicians also felt that the council had done the groundwork for the waterfront successes but been denied the power and money showered on the LDC. But things did happen and the pace was quickened by the fact that the LDC was always living on borrowed time. It was never intended to be permanent but rather was given a five-year contract, meaning that to make any sort of mark it had to press on. The contract was not expected to be renewed but, in the end, it was, for two years only – a decision prompted by the onset of economic recession.

The energy of this cuckoo in the Leeds nest had another far-reaching effect. It produced an equal, but not opposite, reaction from the city council, which set up its own Leeds City Development Company with local business leaders and professionals on the board. This worked with the council's Leeds Development Agency, which was later merged with council engineering,

planning, property and other services to create the Development Department – subsequently renamed 'City Development'. All involved at the time remember a mutual attitude developing between the council and the development corporation of 'anything they can do, we can do better', which was usually to the city's good. Different people in the city award differing credit to the two organisations, but history is likely to see that as a side issue, especially as historians flounder amid the many similar acronyms – LCC, LDC, LCDC, LDA, etc. Between them they were an unprecedentedly powerful engine for 'blue sky' discussion, actual improvement and attracting inward investment. They also galvanised others to join the debate.

The council had been led since May 1980 by an artful politician in the old 'city boss' mode, George Mudie, who was to become Labour MP for East Leeds and, not at all surprisingly in view of his particular talents, deputy chief whip. But in 1989, amid all the regeneration changes, the leadership passed to a young councillor and

27

speed-cycling enthusiast called Jon Trickett, who notched up the pace by several gears. He was from the Left and a union man, but his career as a plumber and builder after leaving Leeds University with a politics MA on top of his Hull politics degree gave him some sympathy with business practicalities. His colleagues on the council included others with an awareness of the importance of bank balances and profit, such as Fabian Hamilton, the future Labour MP for North East Leeds, who ran an organic wine business from the cellars of a mansion in Roundhay as well as a printing firm in a terrace overlooking Woodhouse Moor.

Trickett retained the loyalty of the Mudie core group, but he took a pragmatic approach to the realities of national politics, seeking ways to turn Mrs Thatcher's local government restrictions to Leeds' advantage. The council entered vigorously into competitive bidding for resources and joint public/private projects. One of the first fruits, led by the LDC, on the Board of which were Councillors Brian Walker and Andrew Carter, was an early and very high-profile Private Finance Initiative (PFI) project, the £32,500,000 Royal Armouries Museum, whose austere building by Derek Walker and the Danish architect Henning Larsen opened in 1996. It had a rocky ride in its early years as a lonely outpost in a wasteland dominated by chemical plants, but the council and its partners kept faith and the whole area is now transformed.

The other force changing attitudes in the council's ruling Labour group was that an increasing number of members were relatively young – or at least young at heart. Trickett retained some elements of 'personal rule', but there was a wealth of imagination coming from council members like Bernard Atha (later famous for being escorted by 12 successive Lady Mayoresses during his year as a bachelor Lord Mayor) and Liz Minkin, whose work on planning and urban design

^ Railway Arch infill
RICHARD MORAN / WWW.MORANPHOTO.CO.UK

^ Gilda Porcelli
WWW.JH-JPHOTO.CO.UK

was to earn her an honorary fellowship of the RIBA in 2003. A new notion of Leeds was promoted as a city of fun and sparkle, thronged with students (a population reaching 60,000 when Trickett became council leader), cosmopolitan, a British counterpart to Barcelona. Painfully over-used in the decades since then, the comparison was genuinely fresh and inspiring at the time, especially when the council published rainfall charts which proved that Leeds was actually dryer than the Catalan city. Pavement cafés were encouraged, a movement helped invaluably by Gilda Porcelli, the singing patroness of Pasta Romagna in Albion Place, who attracted much publicity, notably when her outdoor chairs got stuck at crazy angles when genuinely hot sun melted the paving's tar grout. Opera North and the Grand Theatre Trust began the gradual, magnificent transformation of the Grand Theatre, and in 1990 the West Yorkshire Playhouse opened its purpose-built twin theatre on Quarry Hill, the fruit of a genuine community campaign but steered to financial success by civic networking. Councillor Atha, a barrister and actor whose cameo as an accident-prone vicar in Yorkshire TV's soap *Emmerdale* is often repeated on ITV's *It'll Be Alright On the Night*, played a crucial behind-the-scenes role in this cultural surge. At the same time, the 'Queen' of the young-at-heart Labour councillors, grandmother Lorna Cohen, went out clubbing with the London media all night to promote the earliest days of the slogan 'Leeds –

24 hour city', the first place in the country to make that now-routine claim.

There was a lot of hype involved, sustained by a diverse economy which has never been dependent on single, vast but vulnerable, sectors such as steel or wool. But there was a more serious, underlying force at work behind the glitzy change. The 1970s and 80s had seen a slow, debilitating contraction in Leeds' manufacturing sector – once responsible for everything from battle tanks to the Little Nipper mousetrap and Foxtrot-de-Luxe dance-floor polish. Now that decline had been reversed and modern industries were moving in – especially in Information and Communications Technology, or ICT (Trickett coined the phrase 'Intelligent City' in a drive to attract such Internet, computer and wired-society entrepreneurs). In addition service professions, especially in highly skilled and very well-paid fields such as commercial law, were multiplying. Between 1991 and 1997 employment grew by 12 per cent (36,300 extra jobs), double the national figure of 6 per cent and still higher than the 5 per cent regional rise for Yorkshire and the Humber.

The city's new 'Barcelona' strategy and its urban dentistry also had one brilliant architectural inheritance from the 1960s' and early 70s' days of great, grey planning. In the teeth of retailers' opposition and much wider scepticism, the council in 1971 had turned

<< Grand Theatre
© IAN GRUNDY

< West Yorkshire Playhouse
LEEDS LIBRARY AND INFORMATION SERVICES

29

^ Pedestrian precinct
WWW.JH-JPHOTO.CO.UK

almost the whole of Leeds' central core into a traffic-free pedestrian precinct. The idea was driven by the council leader, Frank Marshall, a Conservative with clout who later became minister of local government and a peer, and Geoffrey Thirlwall, Head of Planning. It was a masterstroke, which allowed the rich collection of buildings between the Headrow, Park Row, Briggate and Boar Lane to breathe and be seen – and, in a gradual process over the next 20 years, to preen, as they were restored or enhanced. The precinct's origins lay in Colin Buchanan's seminal Traffic in Towns report published in 1963 by the then Ministry of Transport. The report's enthusiasm for separating cars and pedestrians was promptly siezed upon by Leeds' Labour council, led by Sir Karl Cohen, which obtained a special Parliamentary bill allowing the city to become the first in the country

to implement 'Buchanan measures'. Sir Karl and other far-sighted councillors including Margaret Happold, the Socialist Quaker mother of the architect and engineer Sir Edmund Happold, worked with their officers, notably the city engineer Geoffrey Thirlwall, to prepare the way for the precinct. In accordance with Buchanan's thinking, they also designed its less attractive but essential concomitant, the inner ring road which sweeps the banished traffic through the city centre underground and out of sight.

When the Conservatives regained control in 1967 under Frank Marshall, a politician who later carried out a review of London's government and became a peer, they were equally enthusiastic about the project and saw it through to completion. The perceptive architect and writer Patrick Nuttgens, first director of Leeds

^ Granary Wharf
WWW.JH-JPHOTO.CO.UK

^ St Paul's House
WWW.JH-JPHOTO.CO.UK

Polytechnic (now Leeds Metropolitan University) seemed to foresee the 24-hour city initiative when he entered the new precinct for the first time and exclaimed: 'Astonishingly, you are in the midst, no longer of drab Victorian gloom, but of Victorian vulgarity and fun'. The scheme became a national exemplar for urban planners.

But in wider terms it remained something of a hidden asset, because transitory visitors often passed through Leeds by car through Thirlwall's concrete ravine, or by bus or train, and so never saw it. Non-locals who did penetrate on foot also often found it hard to find their way around. It was not unusual to encounter a stranger who had come to Leeds to try one of Britain's most famous pubs, Whitelock's First City Luncheon Bar, and was about to give up in frustration at ever finding the narrow canyon-like entrance slots to Turk's Head Yard, where it is located.

Again in the face of local opposition, particularly from conservationists and Leeds Civic Trust, the council decided in 1989 that it was time to blow the precinct's trumpet. Outside architects were brought in, Faulkner

Brown from Newcastle, and a delicate but definite structure called Landmark Leeds was imposed on the grid of streets, using Modernist steel gateways, lamp-post banners, distinctive benches and other street furniture, as well as a range of setts and pavement tiles which almost subconsciously guided walkers around. There were serious maintenance problems, and litigation over the contract ended only some 14 years later. But as this concoction settled down it became popular with local people and businesses, and the idea spread. The yards off Lower Briggate lost their long 'Cinderella' status and became chic outriders of the precinct, linking up naturally with the work of the LDC and private developers alongside the riverside Calls and Call Lane. There was another outpost in the Dark Arches, beneath the railway station and by the canal, where a 'souk' of boutiques and stalls was installed and renamed Granary Wharf 'retail festival' by Len Davies, one of a band of innovative property developers with holdings in the city centre. The other side of City Square – a renovation of Sir John Barran's Moorish Victorian fantasy, St Paul's House – set off beautifully the green island of Park

<< Exterior of
  Kirkgate Market
  WWW.JH-JPHOTO.CO.UK

< Interior of
  Kirkgate Market
  WWW.JH-JPHOTO.CO.UK

31

^ Fair at the Town Hall
WWW.JH-JPHOTO.CO.UK

^ Fair at Elland Road
WWW.JH-JPHOTO.CO.UK

> The Light
DLG ARCHITECTS

Square. Most dramatically of all, Queen Victoria Street was roofed by a breathtaking 20th-century version of Leeds' Victorian arcades, including the largest stained-glass canopy in Britain designed by Brian Clarke. Linked to Victoria and Cross Arcades, this became the Victoria Quarter of 'posh' shops, including in 1996 the poshest shop of all. The arrival in Leeds of Harvey Nichols – the personification of London style, and specifically that of Knightsbridge and Princess Diana – was a turning point in outsiders' image of the city, the importance of which cannot be overstated. It had a worthy parallel in the city council's renovation of Kirkgate Market, a 'Turkish Delight' of a building designed by the leading Edwardian architects Leeming and Leeming in 1903–4, which is the largest indoor market in Europe.

At the same time, the council made good use of a strategy of selling property in its own city-centre portfolio that it could not renovate itself because of limited resources. The risk of 'disposing of the family silver' always accompanies such transactions, but Leeds took the view that silver was wasted if simply stashed in a vault – or, in landscape and building terms, left in poor condition with insufficient maintenance and investment. Better to put it on show with a good polish, a top-grade display cabinet and, most important of all, the chance for the public to use it. The Light covered mall off the Headrow and the Electric Press developments are outstanding examples of sale and redevelopment according to enlightened guidelines which give a high priority to the public interest.

These physical changes coincided with further leisure and cultural initiatives dreamed up in what might be

called a 'regenerative spirit', including a vigorous encouragement of floodlighting. Buildings and urban spaces were both suddenly bathed in a mixture of glows, beams and an electric-blue light that became a trademark of night-time Leeds. Victorian cherubs and pediments, all but invisible by day, glowed or were outlined in sharp relief. Drab nooks in the city centre were transformed into mysterious pools of light, and a series of annual Leeds Lighting Awards encouraged imaginative schemes. This also applied to the holding of a Valentine's Fair in the heart of the city in February, often a dull month, which brought roundabouts and a majestic Ferris wheel to Victoria Gardens in front of the Town Hall and Cookridge Street. Like the Leeds Lights in the run-up to Christmas, which are famously but wrongly said to be visible from the moon, the spectacle was relished until the disruptive effects of such central road closures led to its relocation to land beside Leeds United football ground at Elland Road, where it continues to whirl and glow.

All this prosperity and 'zing' attracted increasing numbers of developers, both to nose round the dwindling jigsaw of empty sites and to look at refurbishing old buildings. The process – bringing £4-billion-worth of property investment into Leeds in the 1990s – led to some fine examples of urban dentistry, such as the glass-fronted building at 15/16 Park Row, and interesting transformations of relatively modern but shabby tower blocks such as Minerva House in East Parade and K2 on the corner of Great George Street and Albion Street. The last of these was pivotal to a second great exercise in roofing over an existing street: the creation in 2001 of The Light between the Headrow and

^ Rainbow over Leeds Metropolitan University
WWW.JH-JPHOTO.CO.UK

^ "Leeds in Bloom" flower initiative
WWW.JH-JPHOTO.CO.UK

St Ann Street, a conversion whose arching glass shield over Upper Fountaine Street matches Queen Victoria Street for boldness.

Classic entrepreneurial energy drove such projects, sensing a place unstoppably on the up, but, in another hallmark of the forces driving Leeds, this went in harness with agonising over local planning guidelines and a non-stop architectural debate. John Thorp was involved in this on all fronts, but he was given extra muscle in 1994 by the creation of the Leeds Architecture and Design Initiative. Known universally as LADI (and pronounced 'laddy'), this body sometimes gave architectural discussions in Leeds an air of old-fashioned teachers talking down to the class. LADI was a difficult creature to pin down, but was nonetheless significant as a driver of change. It had no formal executive power (for all that many of those not on it believed that it decided everything). Instead, it was a partnership of different design and development interests in Leeds whose meetings, outings and networking informally maintained the pace which had begun after the arrival of the LDC and the start of Jon Trickett's council leadership.

Like so much of the energy in late-20th-century Leeds, LADI came partly from the vigour of the private sector, constantly pushing, and partly from the council's concern to create partnerships rather than rivalries as the city moved forward. Encouraged by the alternative power base of the LDC, the Leeds Chamber of Commerce had started lobbying in 1989 for more of a say in regeneration. Its move coincided happily with the way that the Conservative government – and increasingly the European Union – was insisting on a partnership element in bids for central funds. So in 1990 an umbrella group, called simply the Leeds Initiative, was set up with a public commitment to joint working. It quickly spawned sub-groups to cover an impressively comprehensive range of subjects; there was even a

Leeds Flower Initiative. Peter Vaughan at the Planning Department had drawn up a blueprint for private/public sector cooperation on urban design and Liz Minkin, one of the young 'Trickett enthusiasts' who was now chair of planning on the council, made the connection with the Leeds Initiative. The new group gave interested outsiders a place at the table and a sense of influence; and although the council's representatives retained control, sometimes rather too obviously, LADI members from all sectors, including the professions and universities, contributed powerfully to the ten-year Vision for Leeds drawn up by the Leeds Initiative in 1999. In a grander version of urban dentistry, the planning section of this document rejected iconic structures in favour of effective strategies for urban transport and sustainability. The council was led throughout this highly innovative period by Brian Walker, a quietly spoken Labour councillor from Rothwell on the southern fringe of the city, who kept a deliberately low profile but got things done. The blueprint was extended by Vision for Leeds II in 2004 and widened, in terms of participation, by the biggest exercise in consultation the city had seen. Developers at the time still felt that their voice was relatively muted – they had only one representative on LADI, albeit a characterful one in the ex-Marxist Peter Connolly. As a result, talks were held between the council, the architect Gordon Carey, the Chamber of Commerce's chief executive Richard Mansell, Kevin Grady of Leeds Civic Trust and LADI's chair Councillor Liz Minkin, which helped lead to the creation of the Leeds Property Forum. Launched in 2003 under the umbrella of the Chamber of Commerce rather than the Leeds Initiative, this promptly set about its mission of 'enabling the property sector to have a voice and be formally engaged in the city'.

In step with its progress went the regular debates within the Leeds Society of Architects and, more publicly, the successful series of talks and discussions originally launched in 2001 by Leeds architect Ian Tod under the title '4X4 Making Places'. Every spring, four evening

^ The Dry Dock
WWW.JH-JPHOTO.CO.UK

gatherings at Leeds Metropolitan University each featured four architects, designers or planning teams who addressed aspects of Leeds (at least initially; the topics have since expanded to Yorkshire and beyond) and then took questions which were often very robust. The classy, almost metropolitan tone of the seminars was encouraged by vigorous 'free-for-alls' afterwards at local restaurants and clubs, or stylish venues such as Gordon Carey's architecture practice headquarters in Rose Wharf, where the future of Leeds was picked apart over a great deal of wine as the sun sank into the Aire.

At the same time there was plenty of hammering at the door by those who sometimes felt excluded. Dr Kevin Grady, the combative director of Leeds Civic Trust, has been a dauntless pin-pricker when LADI showed signs of getting a bit pompous or losing its way. A walking encyclopaedia of Leeds lore, he also spends time at local children's parties in the guise of Dr Marvello the Magician. Significantly his magic, although impressive, is secondary to a bewitching patter. Under his directorship, Leeds Civic Trust has developed into one of the most effective such bodies in the country, with a stack of conferences and reports on such matters as the city's waterfront, licensing policy and heritage buildings to its credit. Peter Connolly, one of Britain's few developers to have spent time in the International Marxist Group, was – and is – another constant believer that the planning process can always be made to work better. He is one of a group who explored the idea of a Leeds

version of Manchester's 'McEnroe Club', a network of movers and shakers who took their nickname after several of them reacted identically to a particularly inane official regeneration slogan with the tennis star's famous cry: 'You cannot be serious!' The Leeds group was to have been called the 'FU Club', because all full Leeds planning applications end with 'FU', a choice of letters often remarked upon. It didn't happen, but the presence of articulate 'ideas people' auditing Leeds while promoting their own, often excellent, ideas has also been crucial to the forces driving change in Leeds. Connolly, for instance, was in the vanguard of waterfront development and brought ashore The Dry Dock, an old Aire and Calder Navigation barge which now serves drinks in a wave-rippled 'sea' of grass opposite the universities.

A couple of years ago, you could sup a pint of locally brewed Tetley's in this landlocked craft, with any Leeds Loiner (the ancient name for locals, coined from our habit of loitering for a gossip at the end of the town's lanes or 'loines') and find them content with the excitements of the 1990s and the changes that Leeds had achieved in time for the Millennium. The sense of optimism, growth, fun and opportunity seemed to be all that a great regional city might wish for its centre. But there was to be no stopping, indeed scarcely even a breathing space. The transformation of Leeds was about to engage a whole set of higher gears.

35

02
TRANSFORMING
THE CITY

Leeds is big and booming, but also a delicate and complex puzzle. Climb to the rooftops and an intricate pattern of gables, mansards, spikes and domes creates a second city in the sky. Below, paved streets, narrow alleys and hidden squares recreate a sense of the old medieval borough. Everything connects, and a great, green girdle of hills and valleys provides a surrounding context to the whole.

ROOFTOP LEEDS

One of the signature tall buildings in Leeds is known, appropriately, as K2. From there one can look down upon the whole length of the Headrow, with the Postmodern Brum confection of BDP's Quarry House to the east and the proud Classicism of Cuthbert Brodrick's Town Hall to the west.

< Leeds University Parkinson Building
and University churches
WWW.JH-JPHOTO.CO.UK

^ Tower Works Campanile
RICHARD MORAN / WWW.MORANPHOTO.CO.UK

Turning a little towards the north, the plain articulated tower of the University of Leeds' Parkinson Building – designed by Lanchester, Lucas and Lodge and completed in 1950 – marks the high ground, beyond which lies Headingley. To the south, in Holbeck, the two mercantile brick campanili of the Tower Works, built by Thomas Shaw in 1864 and by William Bakewell in 1899, can be glimpsed rising on the far side of the railway. In the distance, the gaunt Gothic outlines of Joseph Hansom and Edward Pugin's Mount Saint Mary's Roman Catholic Church of 1852 and 1866 breaks the skyline on Richmond Hill to the southeast. As if to answer the challenge, to the southwest the Anglicans' St Bartholemew's Church, built by Walker and Athron in 1872, rises above the battlements of Armley Prison, first erected by Perkin and Backhouse in 1847 and enlarged a decade later.

Beyond these markers the map of Leeds stretches out,
like a torn tea towel, to Otley, Wetherby, Morley and
Allerton Bywater – but it is in this central area where
Rooftop Leeds can be best experienced. For Rooftop
Leeds is not so much the view from above as the
experience from below, from between tall buildings
where the broken skyline of gables, mansards, spires
and domes protect one from the threatening sky; where
the distant markers define the edge and describe
the destination. For any city that has grown, in the
Industrial and post-Industrial age, from a medieval
street pattern creates its caverns and canyons which
provide that sense of containment in which the eye
is instinctively drawn upwards towards the light.
Here the extraordinary exuberance of Leeming and
Leeming's City Markets of 1904, with their Dutch
gables and Baroque cupolas, provides an object lesson
in architectural precedents, while the white tent-roof
of No.1 City Square, high above City Square, invites
one, like some latter-day Mary Poppins, to sail up in
the glass elevators to a magic world of chimney pots,
parapets and pinnacles.

Most people, when walking through a city, will look
down. They look at the soiled and uneven pavements
so as not to place a foot wrong. They look in the shop
windows to find things they never knew they wanted.
They look at faces and at feet and the in-betweens, but
rarely upwards. But there, on the edge between solid
and void, is a world of architectural expression waiting
to be discovered.

41

At 32 storeys,
Bridgewater Place is
currently the tallest building
in Leeds.

WWW.JH-JPHOTO.CO.UK

BRIDGEWATER PLACE

AEDAS ARCHITECTS LIMITED

Water Lane, Leeds

Construction Value: £85 million
Completion Date: 2007

Description

A new-build mixed-use scheme incorporating 22,000 m² of high-quality office accommodation, 18,500 m² of apartments, 1,400 m² of A1/A3 commercial space (including restaurant, café bar and retail units) and 380 below-ground parking spaces. At 32 storeys, Bridgewater Place is currently the tallest building in Leeds.

History

On the eastern edge of Holbeck, the site has been occupied since the mid-1800s by light industry at its northern end with an expanding mosaic of residential streets to the south. The war years brought the creation of the adjacent Holbeck Munitions Factory, which naturally led to successive redevelopments of the site and area mirroring the country's subsequent growth in industry and commercialism. Homes disappeared, as did the fine grain of Front and Middle Row, and by 1990 the site had become a walled car park.

Client's Brief

The joint-venture client identified the site during the 1990s and approached Aedas towards the end of 1999. Initial market research suggested a group of differing uses would add valuable diversity to the site and surroundings, whilst providing a balanced investment and spreading risk across sectors. Aspirational targets were set at 9,000 m² of offices, a 200-bed hotel and 100 apartments complementing the adjacent financial and headquarters buildings.

Design Process

Early sketches attempted to divide uses into separate buildings surrounding a central space, but the complications of site density, movement and focus left few productive avenues. A more radical approach was needed, which 'stretched the envelope' of commercial design whilst capitalising on the opportunity afforded by the site. The city council's 'tall buildings corridor'

provided that opportunity, and whilst not specifically earmarked for high-rise development the site lay adjacent to a primary southern approach to the city, retained good connectivity with bus and rail routes and could arguably still be classed as central.

Stacking the accommodation released valuable space at low level, creating conditions for public encounter and participation. Breaking the skyline, the structure provided a clear visual marker both for gateway and way-finder aspirations, and its location – visible from City Square and the Headrow – confirmed that high commercial values south of the river were achievable.

But high-rise was not current thinking; only national capitals seemingly warranted such ambition. Yet, with appreciable support from LCC Planning and market growth, the realisation that such strong, confident architecture reflected Leeds' economic direction overcame scepticism. Reframed commercial values recognised the potential of building high, and encouraging optimism in 2000/1 culminated in the start of detailed discussion with Planning and statutory consultees late in 2001.

Through 2002, Leeds enjoyed strengthening financial growth and, as smaller schemes capitalised on sector opportunities, Bridgewater focused on long-term issues. The hotel was dropped in favour of larger office floorplates, additional residential units and improved A1/A3 provisions, with budgets realigned accordingly. The following year saw commercial discussions firm up with Bovis Lend Lease, and by November contracts were signed allowing Bovis to take possession in early 2004. The two and a half year construction phase was procured on a Design and Build basis, with novated architectural and engineering teams.

The architectural composition of the scheme placed emphasis on the vertical metallic tube of the residential

tower facing the city; this 31-storey element, clad in anodised aluminium and glass, reflects the style and chic of city living. The plinth, comprising offices, provides a more restrained yet equally strong horizontal element. More corporate in appearance, this ten-storey base visually grounds the scheme by utilising cast concrete layered with bands of fenestration.

At the heart of the scheme, a nine-storey atrium provides the promised public space, acting as both a sheltered thoroughfare and a distributor for the scheme. As a destination, the atrium provides break-out space for the restaurant, café bar and retail units which surround it; as an enclosure, its volume provides a thermal buffer to more than 25 per cent of the office façade, supplementing the sustainability credentials of the project. Glazed at either end and flooded with light through its ETFE-foil roof, this key space unifies the scheme with the public realm and the urban confidence of Leeds.

The structural solution, comprising post-tensioned flat concrete slabs and reinforced concrete columns, allowed floor-to-floor dimensions to be optimised and negated many of the usual coordination issues. By dramatically reducing the volume of materials and providing in-built acoustic and fire compartmentation, concrete proved to be the natural choice.

Project Sign-off

It could be argued that much of the catalytic effect of Bridgewater Place has already been realised, both locally and across the wider city. High-rise opportunities, and the associated controlling measures, have enjoyed accelerated development over recent years.

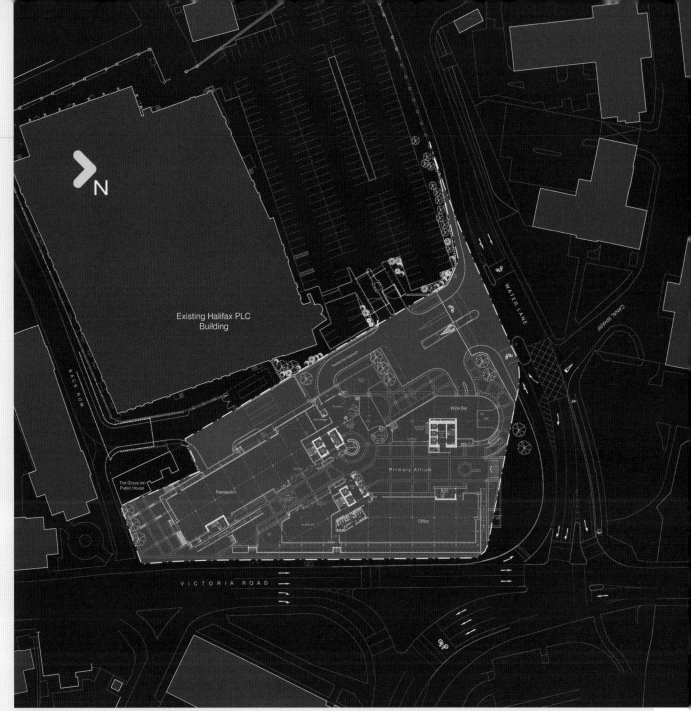

Existing Halifax PLC Building

Wine Bar

Primary Atrium

The Grove Inn Public House

Restaurant

Office

BACK ROW

WATER LANE

CANAL WHARF

VICTORIA ROAD

AEDAS ARCHITECTS LTD

Tall buildings are perhaps the clearest outward expression of a city's own confidence, and the Leeds skyline is punctuated with historic references to its past successes. The addition of Bridgewater Place to that composition is relevant and timely, and Bridgewater will augment people's perception of the size of the city. Many schemes already seek to exceed its height, and in all likelihood the next generation of high-rises will move the definition of 'tall' yet further upwards.

However, fundamentally, Bridgewater is a sophisticated solution to a complex question. Its concept uniquely challenged the norm, and the completed scheme fixes a benchmark for the integration of high-rise schemes into an urban environment.

PROJECT TEAM

Client/Building Owner: **Bridgewater Place Limited**
Architect: **Aedas Architects Limited**
Quantity Surveyor: **AYH Limited**
Structural Engineer: **Connell Mott McDonalds**
Services Engineer: **WSP Group Limited**
Main Contractor: **Bovis Lend Lease PLC**
Fire Consultant: **Arup Fire**
Acoustic Consultant: **Sound Research Laboratory**

The form of the building helps give all its elements a sculptural quality; by introducing non-vertical triangular facets, its elegance and height are reinforced.

LUMIERE

IAN SIMPSON ARCHITECTS

Whitehall Road, Leeds

Construction Value: £150 million
Completion Date: Anticipated 2011

Description

A mixed-use, high-rise, new-build development comprising two towers – one 55 storeys high, the other 33. Lumiere will provide retail units, apartments, commercial offices, a health centre and serviced apartments.

History

Lumiere constitutes the second phase of redevelopment of the former post office site in Leeds' city centre. The plot is bounded on alternate sides by the Park Square Conservation Area and an emerging commercial district. It is near both City Square and Leeds Railway Station, and is at the heart of the southwest corridor into the centre of Leeds.

Client's Brief

The client's main requirement was to provide a landmark project within the centre of Leeds that reflected the aspirations of the client and the city. It was also essential that the quality of the mixed-use spaces provided within the building reflected the potential significance of the project to the city.

Design Process

The premise of proposing Lumiere as a tall building was that it provided two key opportunities. Firstly, it would create a landmark project that would not only provide a point of reference on the Leeds skyline but would also denote arrival within the city centre. Secondly, it gave the opportunity, through the grouping of the accommodation within high-rise elements, of providing a large, covered, publicly accessible space at ground-floor level. This street-level space, or 'Winter Garden', will enable the public to engage with the development at its very heart, provide permeability across the site and is based on Leeds' rich heritage of glass-covered walkways and atria.

The form of the building helps give all its elements a sculptural quality; by introducing non-vertical triangular facets, its elegance and height are reinforced. This accentuates the slenderness of the forms – particularly in the case of the taller of the two towers. As light passes around the building the intention is that these facets should catch it in different ways owing to their orientation, thus reinforcing the sculpted quality of each element.

The siting of a tall building needs to be carefully considered in terms of visual impact and ground-level connections. The design team worked very closely with Leeds City Council to ensure that the proposals were consistent with LCC's emerging tall buildings policy.

Lumiere is to be clad in unitised curtain walling – a system of construction eminently suitable for a glazed building envelope at this height. The composition of the cladding responds to environmental concerns by comprising 50 per cent clear glazed units and 50 per cent 'shadow boxes'. The latter are highly insulated panels that assist in the thermal performance of the building envelope, and incorporate an aluminium sheet directly behind the glass that can be coloured to suit the façade. Ian Simpson Architects wanted to make the coloration of these panels specific to Leeds and the site context. They noted the strong Moorish architectural precedent within the buildings of Park Square and elsewhere in Leeds, and decided to colour the shadow boxes with a geometrical patterning system reflecting this influence. The arrangement of the patterning also helps to add weight to the base of the buildings and lightness to the top, thus reinforcing the height and perspective of the two towers. The difference of the base colours to those of the shadow boxes on each building helps accentuate the form and outline of the individual towers when set visually against one another.

The principal structure of both towers is post-tensioned concrete slabs with slip-formed concrete cores, while the Winter Garden at ground-floor level is formed of steel. The main constraint upon the engineers was to provide a rigid frame to the slender tower-forms while maximising space and headroom. Post-tensioned slabs provide rigid, slim floorplates that fulfil this criterion. The other consideration was accommodating the movement between the towers and the Winter Garden – inevitable when such large forms adjoin a glazed atrium.

The construction is carefully sequenced to ensure that activities such as the cores and floorplates are closely followed by the building envelope, to help ensure rapid and efficient resolution of the project.

Project Sign-off

Lumiere will be one of the tallest residential buildings in Europe when finished. The construction of such a project is indicative of the aspiration, confidence and spirit of progress within Leeds. The unique sculpted and slender form of Lumiere is indicative of the city's emphasis upon high-quality design and innovation. Its connection with the street level, and the provision of publicly accessible space at its heart, means that this is a development that is not only based on the architectural precedents and heritage of Leeds but is something that its citizens can truly engage with and enjoy.

PROJECT TEAM

Client/Building Owner: **Lumiere LP**
Executive Architect: **Brewster Bye Architects**
Architect: **Ian Simpson Architects**
Quantity Surveyor: **Burnley Wilson Fish**
Structural Engineer: **WSP Buildings**
Services Engineer: **WSP Buildings and Silcock Leedham LLP**
Main Contractor: **Carillion PLC**

To ensure the delivery of a high-quality façade, Permasteelisa –
a world leader in curtain walling –
was selected to design, fabricate and
install the building envelope.

PRINCES EXCHANGE
CAREYJONES ARCHITECTS

Aire Street, Leeds

Construction Value: £13.5 million
Completion Date: December 1999

Description
These new-build city-centre commercial offices were
originally designed speculatively, but incorporated
minor modifications to suit a major pre-let tenant
(taking 70 per cent of the building) before construction
commenced.

History
The brownfield site was formerly occupied by railway
sheds, with its last use being for rail-customer parking
and the Red Star Parcels delivery firm. After clearing,
the site now faces the new North Concourse entrance
to Leeds City Station and is highly visible from the
main Leeds–London railway line. It is also particularly
prominent from the central City Square.

Client's Brief
Client aspirations were for an international-standard
landmark office building that would take full advantage
of its city-centre site and attract a suitably high-
profile occupier. Given the speculative nature of the
development, the design was required to observe the
market trends prevalent at the time (the building was
originally designed in 1992).

Design Process
The cleared site presented a number of constraints,
most notably that of having no 'front' or 'back'. The
site presents itself to Aire Street, City Square, Leeds
City Station, the river and riverside walkway and also a
pedestrian route to the railway station. This suggested
that the proposal should have no discernible rear
elevation, the whole presenting the image of a very
high-quality modern building.

Original design proposals saw an 18-storey tower
providing a strong focus and visual stop to the
southwest corner of City Square, whilst also respecting

the concept of 'no rear elevation'. The tower proposals were initially discussed with Leeds Development Corporation (LDC) before being presented to the Royal Fine Art Commission in London. The RFAC urged that the building be shortened. Subsequent review reduced its height to eight floors of accommodation, with undercroft parking beneath and plant accommodation above.

Extensive research was undertaken, in both Paris and London, on a suitable precedent for the project. This inspired a predominantly glass building that created public open spaces, including external plaza areas to both the station and river frontage, to encourage and engage with pedestrian movement.

With much of the railway station being built over the river on Victorian arches, an additional constraint was placed upon the siting of this building – that of ensuring that all foundations hit solid ground, a requirement of the funding institutions. Respecting this requirement saw the building designed with its core providing a visual focus to City Square and the floorplates arranged either side, filling the land between Aire Street and the river retaining wall. As such, the eastern floorplate terminates on plan at a 45° point – a feature initially resisted by the letting agents, but one which ultimately became the signature of the development and which is accordingly highlighted in most publicity shots of the building.

To ensure the delivery of a high-quality façade, Permasteelisa – a world leader in curtain walling – was selected to design, fabricate and install the building envelope. A major influence on its design was the fact that the system was prefabricated and then hung on the building in 3 by 4 m panels, providing a factory-assembled level of build quality.

Extensive research and testing was undertaken with Permasteelisa on the appearance of the building, in order to ensure the correct specification for the glazed vision and non-vision panels, together with all other façade features. Numerous samples were viewed on site in conjunction with Leeds City Planners before the final selection was made.

The core was designed to reflect the elements within it – specifically the position of the lifts. It had been intended that the lift lobby would present the user with stunning views across City Square when exiting the elevators. However, tenant preference revised this proposal in favour of locating the lifts closer to the office entrances, requiring a modest redesign.

The building is based on a 9 by 9 m structural-steel grid, with composite-deck floors. It has a 2.7 m floor-to-ceiling height, with 4 m floor to floor, and the facility for subdivision and cellularisation on a 1.5 m grid.

Initial design commenced in February 1992, with LDC approval being received in August of that year. Subsequent lengthy price negotiations concluded in February 1998, and a start was made on site in August 1998. Completion was achieved in December 1999.

Project Sign-off

Princes Exchange, along with the North Concourse contract, was a catalyst for redevelopment on the banks of the River Aire upstream. The projects have made this area a destination in itself rather than simply a passageway to the rail station.

This overall development involved a large number of private and public bodies working together to achieve a major improvement in the environment around Leeds City Station, and so in the very heart of the city itself. Its success can be gauged by the fact that the retail units within the Concourse and the office building remain fully occupied.

PROJECT TEAM

Client/Building Owner: **Teesland Development (Northern) Limited**
Architect: **careyjones architects**
Quantity Surveyor: **Michael Eyres**
Structural Engineer: **WSP (formerly HJT Consulting Engineers)**
Services Engineer: **William E Hannen & Associates**
Main Contractor: **Kier Northern Limited**
Steelwork Fabricator: **Wescol Glosford plc**
Façade Engineer: **Permasteelisa**

The retention of the tower structure afforded careyjones architects the opportunity to capitalise on its existing identity and maintain its height, whilst redeveloping the surrounding site.

WEST CENTRAL
CAREYJONES ARCHITECTS

Royal Mail House, Wellington Street, Leeds

Construction Value: £72 million
Completion Date: October 2005

Description

The scheme involved the partial demolition and redevelopment of the Royal Mail tower, and the construction of two new residential wings, a podium car park and a new piazza.

History

Royal Mail House has been a dominant presence on Wellington Street since its completion in the 1970s, and it is a landmark on the city skyline. The competition-winning new scheme aimed to retain the presence of the original building whilst developing it in the context of the changing cityscape of Leeds' 'West End'.

Client's Brief

The brief was to maximise the potential accommodation on the site. Crucial to this aim was the provision of residents' parking and large commercial units with frontages to a new public piazza which would separate the buildings from the planned second phase of the project. The site was identified as a key 'gateway' to Leeds city centre, and one that should be celebrated.

Design Process

The retention of the tower structure afforded careyjones architects the opportunity to capitalise on its existing identity and maintain its height, whilst redeveloping the surrounding site. The T-form plan that evolved to maximise the potential for residential accommodation on the plot, but also to stabilise the existing structure, was a fundamental design concept that was pivotal throughout the development of the scheme, from inception to construction. Additional new-build wings were orientated to achieve optimum views to and from the building from the key arterial routes in Leeds. To this end, careyjones architects endeavoured to ensure that the gable ends of these wings were predominantly glazed in order to maximise views from the residential units, but also

to present 'active' façades to the city throughout the day. Key to the architectural expression of the scheme was the clear material identity of the individual design elements: the existing tower, the new wings, the vertical circulation and the podium car park.

The architects opted to use brick as the main cladding material on the new-build portion of the scheme to reflect the dominant architectural expression on Wellington Street and the adjacent Conservation Area. Whilst they originally proposed that this be stack bonded, thus expressing modern building technology, they reverted to traditional bonded brickwork as the development of the cost plan and programme led to issues with this construction type. The existing structure would not support a traditional brick skin – or, indeed, any cladding of weight – and thus a lightweight terracotta-tile rainscreen construction was chosen for it. The architects worked to ensure that the tile chosen had a module size comparable to the adjacent brick coursing, and that it reflected the scale of the structure whilst maintaining the organic expression of the brick. They clad the main vertical circulation with a metal rainscreen to clearly identify the change in use and also to enrich the architectural expression.

The undulating podium-car-park wall bounding Northern Street was clad in blue engineering brick with expressed courses, this complementary material providing the robust base desired in juxtaposition to the 'free-form' expression.

Careyjones won the competitive tender for the scheme in 1999 and submitted the original planning application for the overall site in 2000, receiving permission in early 2001. They subsequently submitted a revised application to suit the aspirations of building owners, K W Linfoot Plc, in 2004. Construction started on site in August 2003,

ALL IMAGES ON THIS SPREAD COURTESY OF CAREYJONES ARCHITECTS LTD

shell and core works were completed in October 2005 and the scheme was handed over to fit-out contractors who completed their work by May 2006.

Throughout the development of the scheme, careyjones worked closely with Leeds Planning and Building Control Departments to ensure that all aspirations for the scheme were met. Whilst compromise has sometimes been necessary, the overall process has been positive and has resulted, the architects believe, in a building that represents closely the original images developed as part of their competition-winning information back in 1999.

Project Sign-off

Since this project was conceived and started on site, the surrounding western area of central Leeds has redeveloped radically.

The aspiration was always that this scheme should be a generator of and gateway to the developing West End of the city. Adjacent development sites – such as West Riverside and Wellington Place – have been masterplanned and, to some extent, developed from this premise, improving the activity and vitality of this emerging city quarter.

The West Central scheme maintains its landmark status in the evolving skyline, thus enhancing its presence as a key gateway building within the city. Furthermore, the ensuing development of the Phase 2 site will serve to augment this architecturally exciting and prominent site within Leeds city centre.

It is planned that this development will remain an important landmark building within Leeds for the foreseeable future – an indicator of the potential to develop existing buildings into new and inspiring developments, thereby enhancing the vibrancy of the city.

PROJECT TEAM

Client/Building Owner: **Scarborough Development Group (formerly Teesland/Sterling Capitol) / K W Linfoot Plc**

Residential Client: **K W Linfoot Plc**

Architect: **careyjones architects**

Quantity Surveyor: **Michael Eyres**

Structural Engineer: **WSP (formerly HJT Consulting Engineers)**

Services Engineer: **Hammonds**

Main Contractor: **Shepherd Construction Limited**

^ Rural Leeds
WWW.JH-JPHOTO.CO.UK

> Adam Interior,
Harewood House
WWW.JH-JPHOTO.CO.UK

OPEN SPACE
LEEDS

Most of Leeds is open space. Garforth and
Swillington and Kippax are surrounded by
rolling fields, which make the city seem very
distant. From Collingham to Otley the rural
ride is almost uninterrupted, except perhaps
by the great estate of Harewood House.
But Open Space Leeds is largely an urban
phenomenon, an experience of contrast and
containment in which proud buildings stand
back to expose themselves before the city
closes in again beyond them.

^ Harewood House
WWW.JH-JPHOTO.CO.UK

However, it should be allowed that Harewood House,
with its Robert Adam interiors of 1765 and Charles
Barry exterior of 1843, and Temple Newsam, largely
'Jacobethan' but altered later, achieve the same effect
magnificently in their Capability Brown landscapes.

Consider Cuthbert Brodrick's Corn Exchange of
1861. Here is a Victorian colosseum where merchant
gladiators would fight over the price of grain behind
walls of millstone grit as robust as any medieval

^ Temple Newsam
WWW.JH-JPHOTO.CO.UK

54

ERECTED. A.D. 1862.

˄˄ Corn Exchange
WWW.JH-JPHOTO.CO.UK

˄ Cuthbert Brodrick's
pioneering Corn Exchange
LEEDS LIBRARY AND
INFORMATION SERVICES

fortress. And around this fulcrum, the streetscape turns from Duncan Street into New Market Street. Without its presence, the urban experience would be all the poorer, for the Corn Exchange makes that space and demands attention of itself.

At the top of Kirkgate, Reginald Blomfield's Headrow development of 1924 cut a line through the city from Victoria Square to Quarry Hill, creating an edge of fine 'Wrenaissance' buildings which once ushered the traffic along towards Blomfield's rond point petrol station for Appleyard's garages, now the Eastgate Fountain, at one end. These great walls of silence, more suited to Hampton Court Palace than a commercial thoroughfare, rise and fall, holding the city back along their length. But at the junction of Cookridge Street – in a series of complex, stepped moves – Open Space Leeds reveals itself as Victoria Square. First there is the polished granite façade of Jeremy Dixon and Edward Jones's

Henry Moore Institute, completed in 1993 and a skilful sleight of hand which turns a dull, repetitive Victorian terrace into an urban statement. An elegant, arched bridge, also theirs, connects to the new-ish City Art Gallery which extends from the Municipal Buildings, built by W. H. Thorp in 1887. Although these represent an uncomfortable collision of a modern façade with a Second Empire palace, they nevertheless provide an open space set back from the traffic which prepares one for the civic grandeur and sheer hubris of Brodrick's Town Hall, surely the best 19th-century building in Yorkshire. What if that dome had never been built? So proud are the Corinthian columns that the Town Hall would still have stood, as the choir sang when the foundation stone was laid, 'a trophy to Freedom, to Peace, and to Trade'. No wonder Queen Victoria spent two days in Leeds when she opened the Town Hall in September 1858.

The key requirement of the brief was that the square should be able to accommodate 5,000 people safely and, with in-built technology and facilities, to enable a wide variety of events to be staged.

PHOTO COURTESY OF LEODIS.NET

MILLENNIUM SQUARE
LEEDS CITY COUNCIL

Cookridge Street, Calverley Street, Great George Street, Leeds

Construction Value: £12 million
Completion Dates: Millennium Square
Phase I – December 2000
Phase II – April 2001
Perimeter Building Projects – August 2008

Description

A new civic and public events space created from 1960s demolition sites and by the closure of streets. The scheme includes the relocation of the city's Mandela Garden.

History

The site is at the heart of the civic quarter – an area where the city expanded dramatically in the Victorian era to the northwest of its historic centre. New streets were laid out, back-to-back houses built and major public buildings constructed – including the 1858 Town Hall by Cuthbert Brodrick. Demolitions of houses and a swimming pool created sites for the 1933 Civic Hall and a late 1960s temporary car park.

Client's Brief

The client's brief was formed by Leeds City Council as the basis for a Millennium Lottery Bid. The Millennium Commission had a major input into the brief as the scheme evolved, especially in support of the unique events space concept and the revitalisation of, and access to perimeter buildings. The key requirement of the brief was that the square should be able to accommodate 5,000 people safely and, with in-built technology and facilities, to enable a wide variety of events to be staged. There was also a requirement that a quiet garden area should be created and include a water feature and public art. This became the new Mandela Garden.

The City Council owned land and buildings around the proposed square. Its ambition was to generate an increase in financial and cultural value of these properties as a result of the construction of the square and thereby enable some disposals to fund the Council's element of the costs of the project.

Design Process

The project was initiated by the removal of two streets, thereby taking traffic away from the portico entrance of the Civic Hall and from the north–south spine of the new space. A third street, Cookridge Street was closed to traffic and paved. Vehicular access was retained for emergencies only. Statutory services were moved to the perimeters of the square to ensure that no future access to them would disturb the surfaces or operation of the square.

The space is L-shaped, slopes gently southwards and has eight entrances from adjacent streets. This led to the creation of a dynamic space rather than an enclosed square. However two of the major buildings fronting it are of symmetrical design – the Civic Hall and the Leeds Mechanics Institute. The latter has become the new City Museum. These civic buildings generated two key axes which intersect at the centre of the stage area on the square. To emphasise these formal axes, obelisks and gilded 'art-deco' owls – derived from the Civic Hall architecture – were placed on the square either side of the Civic Hall portico. Pairs of cast iron lanterns reproduced from Brodrick's originals, together with trees and planters, were set out to emphasise the axis of the Leeds Institute building.

The need for the space to be fully accessible to all and to have good performance sightlines ruled out terracing and interconnecting flights of steps. As a positive result of the requirements of its events usage, the square slopes evenly from north to south, following the natural contours.

The need for the space to readily accommodate a wide variety of different activities such as concerts, an ice rink or Christmas and Easter markets meant that space had to be found to accommodate a demountable stage and public toilet facilities. This resulted in a series of underground storage, technical support, toilet and changing areas (six changing rooms, toilets, showers,

kitchen and canteen, green room, plant rooms, storage and workshops).

Because of the need on occasions to host major events with large numbers of people, the surface of the square is largely paved – in Yorkstone flags divided into a large grid by granite paving strips. Paving strips are also used to guide the visually impaired through the space. Inset into the paving are drainage slots, bronze sockets for the erection of events fencing and gates and a network of accessible service ducts for lighting, power and communications cabling.

The stage area is flat and accommodates the demountable covered stage structure. This is placed on the diagonal and the audience fans out from it on a 1 in 20 slope, affording good sightlines. Triangular staircase enclosures and a circular lift shaft service the below-stage changing, canteen and technology rooms. The lift lands both at paving level and stage level. Ducts carry cables from technology rooms to a front-of-stage control point and then to a services and safety control tower at the northeast corner of the square. This contains a dedicated electrical substation for the civic quarter and the square. The ducts also connect to the perimeter sound and lighting masts which direct sound into the space rather than on to the faces of perimeter buildings. The tower was transformed by an attached sculpture created by Richard Wilson and funded by the Henry Moore Foundation. The services tower is attached to a terrace which looks out over the square. Beneath this are permanent toilet facilities to serve an audience of 5,000 people. The terrace walls and the faces of planters and other terraces around the square are clad in green granite. Bespoke seats and litter bins are in stainless steel and bronze.

Seats, trees and planters are located at the edges of the events 'arena', whilst the Mandela Garden is intensively planted. In contrast to the large open events space this more intimate garden area – rededicated by Nelson Mandela at the formal opening – was created in the south-west corner of the square. It includes fountains and the city's 2006 award-winning garden from the Chelsea Flower Show. It also includes the sculpture *Both Arms* by the Leeds-born sculptor Kenneth Armitage.

The City Council achieved its aim of funding the costs of the square by disposals or development of the key corner and perimeter sites. In a clockwise sequence, these

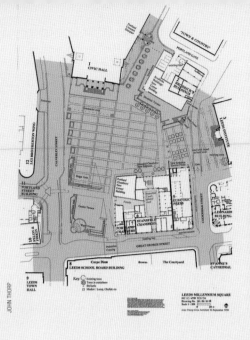

projects begin with Brodrick's buildings which contain two bars / cafés and apartments forming the northeast edge of the square.

The eastern face of the square is formed by the Leeds Institute building. A new City Museum has been created here as a result of a successful bid to the Heritage Lottery Fund. The Leonardo Building closes the southeast corner of the square and contains offices and the Council's City Development Planning 'one-stop-shop'.

Forming the southern face of the square are The Electric Press, Stansfeld Chambers and Portland Chambers buildings. These, as a whole group of buildings, house the Leeds Met University Film and Media school, The Carriageworks Theatre and a variety of bars and restaurants. Internal restoration and construction of an arcade and glazed roofed courtyard were part-funded by the Millennium Commission to secure public access to and through this group of buildings – a factor critical to the vitality of the square.

A BBC outdoor screen was designed to fit the north elevation of the new theatre building. This complex project was the result of a competitive Millennium bid process led by the Council and it became a successful public/private sector partnership project. The Portland Street building enclosing part of the south-west corner of the square contains a restaurant and apartments. This was created through a site disposal by the council. Its curved corner responds to the 1930s Brotherton wing of the Leeds General Infirmary (as does that of the Leonardo Building at the southeast corner). This wing and the Civic Hall complete the diverse set of buildings which define the perimeter of the square. The Town Hall and former Leeds School Board buildings give a powerful Victorian focus to the views out of the square to the south. The Town Hall tower and the Civic Hall spires create the dominant skyline features of the perimeter of Millennium Square.

Project Sign-off

The square and its perimeter buildings have evolved over a 12-twelve year period. The range of events which have taken place in the Square over the past decade have been remarkable for their diversity. Civic, community, cultural and commercial events have been successfully undertaken and further enriched as perimeter buildings have come into use. The experience of the project has informed the creation of a wide range of public realm projects including City Square, Briggate and city centre street works. The creation of a large, complementary green space is the city's next ambition.

PROJECT TEAM

Client/Building Owner: **Leeds City Council**

Design: **Leeds Civic Architect, Leeds City Council's Highway Agency and Design Services Agency**

Architects: **Leeds Civic Architect**

Specialist Sub-contractors: **Gilded bronze owl sculptures and casting of Kenneth Armitage's "Both Arms" - Paul Dimishky**

General Contractors: **Birse**

The design of the new Millennium Square responded to the axis of the Museum building to create a dignified setting for it. Along the axis are placed the steps, ramps, landings and terraces which front the building.

LEEDS CITY MUSEUM
AUSTIN SMITH LORD

Millennium Square, Leeds

Construction Value: £20 million - including fit-out
Completion Date: 12 September 2008

Description
The creation of a new City Museum by the renovation and conversion of the former Leeds Mechanics Institute, a grade II* listed building by Cuthbert Brodrick.

History
Between 1858 and 1888 most of the key civic buildings of Victorian Leeds were constructed in this north-western area of the expanding city centre. The Leeds Mechanics Institute was completed within a new street pattern in 1865.

The new setting of the building is Millennium Square, inaugurated in 2001.

Client's Brief
Originally, the museum was housed in the premises of the Leeds Philosophical and Literary Society. Following bomb damage during the Second World War, temporary museum and storage facilities were created in several locations.

After many feasibility studies of organisational and spatial requirements, and of existing and new building sites, the City Council commenced a process of forming a Stage 1 Lottery Bid in 2000.

The City Council owned the Leeds Institute Building which housed the Civic Theatre and facilities for the College of Music. Both these users were provided with new accommodation. Of particular significance was the evolution of the Civic Theatre into the new Carriageworks Theatre, also facing onto and enlivening the new Millennium Square.

The other key decision was to create a separate storage, conservation, educational and visitor centre for the city's collections – the new 'Discovery Centre' located close to the Royal Armouries Museum.

Thus the brief for the Leeds Institute Building was to repair, conserve and adapt its remarkable fabric and principal spaces and, on three levels, to produce display, visitor, servicing and full access facilities for a City Centre Museum.

Design Process
The central design challenges at all stages of the 8 year programme for the project were: the restoration and adaptation of the splendid drum-like central space and its 'horseshoe' balcony; the restoration and adaptation of the grand entrance space and adjacent original lending library; the resolution of complex access and spatial arrangements created by the original plans and cross-sections of the building; good accessibility for all visitors and practical service arrangements within a tight Victorian street pattern; repair and restoration of the overall fabric of the building, including its splendid exterior.

The response to these challenges was to work closely with advisors to the Heritage Lottery Fund, with English Heritage and many consultees in order to balance repairs, adaptations and conservation work with all the requirements of a vibrant, accessible and environmentally stable museum.

The City Museum building is both II* listed and forms part of a conservation area containing Grade I, II* and II listed buildings.

The design of the new Millennium Square responded to the axis of the Museum building to create a dignified setting for it. Along the axis are placed the steps, ramps, landings and terraces which front the building.

Further into the square, a symmetrical arrangement of ornate cast iron lamps (cast from two originals) and granite clad tree and shrub planters.

62

ED WARING

The roadway which crosses the front of the Museum was closed to traffic to enhance this setting.

A new access ramp to the main entrance was very carefully designed in relation to basement windows and a new café terrace on the southern end of the frontage is given access from the building by the forming of new doorways from existing window openings. For these, new matching Millstone Grit stonework was carved to match existing basement detailing.

The new museum is named in gilt letters to match the 1865 'Leeds Institute' title high upon the frontage of the building. Above this, the setting of the frontage is completed by the recreation of a missing cast iron 'crown' to the top of the tapering roof form above the central bay.

This completes the restoration of the French 'second Empire' character of Brodrick's original design.

The north and east elevations, facing former or surviving back streets were plainer than the more civic fronts to the south and west. These locations have readily accommodated service delivery and group access points.

It has also been easier to create black-out conditions for certain gallery spaces behind the windows of these elevations and to incorporate service lifts and other supportive spaces to the principal museum display spaces.

The roof elements of the building include conical forms above the central 'drum' and a truncated, steep-faced pyramid over the main entrance. The restoration of the latter included fine "fish-scale" slate work and the conical shapes were re-slated with great skill on tightly radiussed forms.

Internally, the grand Victorian spaces – entrance hall and staircases, central auditorium and L-shaped former

subscription library – have been restored to re-establish the strong character and detailing of Brodrick's original spaces.

In the entrance space lift arrangements have been discreetly installed to connect multiple levels and principal floors directly from the main entrance. The colouration relates directly to Brodrick's bold and idiosyncratic architectural detailing.

A key design decision was to make the architectural detailing and materials of new interventions clean and simple to complement Brodrick's work. Hence, plain oak, glass and stainless steel have been included throughout the building for such elements as new doors, built-in seating, a new public staircase.

The restoration of the central 'drum' structure involved, first the structural element of its basement space. From a single cast iron column at the centre of its circular plan, twelve beams radiate to the solid masonry of the perimeter wall. Just inset from this wall cast iron columns extend upwards to support the horse-shoe shaped, stepped and seated viewing balcony which surrounds the central auditorium. This space has been restored as an open, versatile space for events, displays, talks, etc.

It is crowned by the surviving gasolier and extract ventilation structure. Around the walls of the space areas of surviving Minton Hollins tiling have been framed to indicate the decorative practicality of the original finishes to this space.

The most revealing architectural intervention is at first floor level on the western, entrance side of the building. Here a flat leaded roof surrounding the central drum has been cut through with a crescent-shaped roof light.

This reveals the external shape of the 'drum', its original circle of sash windows below the eaves of the conical roof

ALL PHOTOS ON THIS SPREAD BY TIM GREEN

and also lights the several access doors to the auditorium balcony.

Linked to this is a new oak, glass and steel staircase set beneath the pyramidal roof which crowns the entrance face of the museum.

The remarkable timber framed structure which supports this roof-form is left exposed and is of almost medieval character.

It illustrates the structural ingenuity in all of Brodrick's great Leeds works. This characteristic is also found in the inventive laminated and composite trusses which span the gallery spaces of the top floor of the museum.

The crucial interventions to the building have included the insertion of floors across former tall studio spaces and across half-level changes which originally confused the cross-sectional arrangement of the building. These interventions have also been used to facilitate services distribution.

The diversity and complexity of the fit out of the project and of support spaces such as the café and museum shop has formed the third element of design approaches to this scheme. Its diversity and complexity have nevertheless been woven carefully into the Brodrick restoration and the contemporary architectural interventions so that all three elements combine into a singular museum experience.

Project Sign-off

The client, architectural, technical, museum and constructional teams have worked together across a period of eight years. There is a sense of richness and coherence in the building which derives from that long, positive association of skills across a challenging project. The museum crowns a twelve year civic endeavour to establish a new cultural presence in the projects which surround Millennium Square and which form a new Civic Quarter.

The project has already become a vibrant 'place' – inside and out – within the evolving cultural life of the city.

PROJECT TEAM

Client/Building Owners: **Leeds City Council**

Architect: **Austin Smith Lord**

Conservation Architect: **Lloyd Evans Prichard**

Architect: **Stage 1 Lottery Bid and Liaison – Leeds Civic Architect**

Fit out design: **Redman Design**

Quantity Surveyor: **Walfords**

Structural and Services Engineer: **Buro Happold**

Project Manager: **Turner & Townsend**

Contractor: **Laing O'Rourke**

Fit-out contractor: **Beck Interiors**

The first response to this complex brief was
to ensure that floor levels and circulation
arrangements of the old and new elements
of the Leonardo building linked to one
another and to the adjacent Thoresby
building. This would allow a diversity of
adaptable office accommodation.

THE LEONARDO BUILDING
LEEDS CIVIC ARCHITECT

2 Rossington Street LS2 8HD

Construction Value: £3.5 million
Completion Date: 1998

Description

The building is formed of two connected elements: the conversion of a late 19th century listed former printing works and a new extension filling an adjacent open site.

History

The Civic Quarter of Leeds includes a single city block formed of two Victorian/Edwardian school buildings and a Victorian printing works. The latter is called the Leonardo Building, built in 1892 as a colour-lithographic printing works. The buildings were vacated in 1993.

Client's Brief

The client was the City Council's office and facilities accommodation group. Working in liaison with the Education Department, a new replacement high school was created in the inner city closer to students' homes.

The original Leonardo building had also been used for teaching purposes and so the whole building group, playgrounds and an open yard alongside the former printing works became available at the same time.

The client's brief was to create public access to information and advisory services on a single site and provide supporting office accommodation. The 'one-stop-shop' arrangements were to be clearly accessible to visitors and children's play facilities provided.

The brief for the 'Leonardo' element of this 90,000 sq ft project included planning, development and economic services information facilities, adaptable office accommodation, a small rooftop terrace – to encourage this approach on other projects – and a distinctive meeting room for council, stakeholder or partnership groups.

The building was to be adaptable to future changes of use, to respond to conservation area and restoration challenges in an exemplary way, to visually strengthen

the open street corner where Cookridge and Rossington Streets intersect and, simultaneously define one of several 'corners' of the emerging Millennium Square project.

Design Process

The first response to this complex brief was to ensure that floor levels and circulation arrangements of the old and new elements of the Leonardo building linked to one another and to the adjacent Thoresby building. This would allow a diversity of adaptable office accommodation.

To achieve this in plan and section the levels of both old and new elements of the building connected to two new staircases. These were provided in the earlier conversion works of the Thoresby building in anticipation of the Leonardo project.

A central stair, lift, toilets, showers and services structure connects the elaborate architectural language of the printing works and the new corner building.

From basement to roof, the listed building has five levels; the new structure rises two more floors above the old.

The top floor of the new building contains responses to the brief for a distinctive meeting room and for a roof terrace. These indoor and outdoor spaces look down on to part of Millennium Square and provide close-ups of Victorian roofs, domes and the distinctive 'Electric Press' chimney. The circular meeting room provides long distance views of skylines and the tree-covered ridges which characterise inner Leeds.

An inner courtyard, formed in part by historic glazed brick walls, provides a naturally lit and ventilated inner perimeter to the buildings. At ground level the space offers sheltered cycle storage. With this facility and generous showers, 'cycle-to-work' is a well-used

THE LEONARDO BUILDING

opportunity provided by the Leonardo Building.

The top floor of the existing building, including the upper levels of the corner tower, was carefully restored to reflect its north-lit, historic use as a lithographic studio for the printing works. Material produced here has been found and copies are currently being made to display inside the Leonardo building.

Exposed pine trusses and beams and cast iron columns form the exposed Victorian structure of the old printing works.

Internally, the new extension has exposed brick and blockwork – painted or sprayed to reflect the industrial character of this location.

The external forms and planes as well as the skyline of the Leonardo building were derived from a careful reading of the street patterns resulting from sequential Victorian decisions on which street line to set rectangular or square school buildings. In the case of the Leonardo building, the walls follow oblique angled street lines.

In the design of the new building, it was decided to play on these two geometries by having principal wall planes following the street lines whilst introducing deep, oblique recesses to the façade with window panels parallel to stepped building planes.

These decisions were given emphasis by the use of new-red-sandstone string courses set into local sandstone cladding.

A bold curved corner of stone work contains 'slot' windows – vertical and horizontal – which, from within, frame random or composed views of adjacent buildings and spaces. The curved corner leads to the public entrance to the building.

The new roof terraces and circular corner room make references to the 1930s Brotherton wing of the Leeds General Infirmary located on the western side of Millennium Square.

This Portland stone-clad building has south-facing semi-circular balconies in 'ocean-liner' style. There is a deliberate reference to this in the treatment of the roof terrace, the circular meeting room and in the curved corner of the building.

Although the Leonardo Building was completed at the moment of the commencement of Millennium Square, it's corner composition introduced the challenge of addressing several different corner conditions created by the Millennium Square Project.

The Leonardo Building offers a new south corner setting for the City Museum – housed in the adjacent 1865 Mechanics Institute by Cuthbert Brodrick.

A neutral grey bay containing service spaces forms a transition to the elaborately detailed existing building.

The boldest element of the 1892 building is a square corner tower set obliquely to create a bold corner to Cookridge Street and Great George Street.

It was originally crowned with a lead-covered 'baroque' dome which was removed in the 20th century.

In order to re-assert the existing building's corner setting and restore a lost component of the skyline, a 'corona' was created, inspired by other Leeds examples.

With this skyline gesture, the careful re-slating of roofs, the repair and cleaning of the bold grit-stone brick structure of the old Leonardo building, the character of the former printing works was fully revealed.

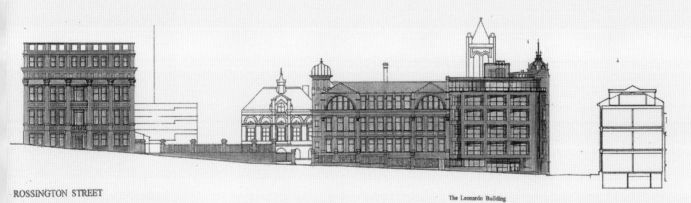

ROSSINGTON STREET

The Leonardo Building

LEEDS CIVIC ARCHITECT

The new corona, a new lift motor room with attached flues, the Electric Press chimney and the copper-clad ventilation domes of the adjacent Thoresby Building together form a skyline group seen from several view points.

Project Sign-off

The 'Leonardo' scheme, together with the refurbishment and complementary re-use of the adjacent Victorian schools, became a catalytic project for the wider regeneration of the Civic Quarter.

There followed the Millennium Square project, the restoration and extension of St Anne's Cathedral, and the large-scale 'K2' and 'The Light' projects. These have illustrated how enlightened partnership working between diverse client groups together with creative asset management can lead to rich dynamic and coherent revitalisation of large parts of a city such as Leeds.

PROJECT TEAM

Architect: **Leeds Civic Architect**

Interior Designers, Quantity Surveyors, Structural Mechanical & Electrical Engineers, Clerks of Works & Service Inspectors, Planning Supervisors: **Design Services Agency – Leeds City Council**

General Contractors: **Phase I (structural refurbishment) Wildgoose Construction Ltd. Phase II (new build and servicing and finishing of Phase I) M J Gleeson Group.**

Specialist Sub-contractors & Suppliers:
**Stone – Johnsons Wellfeild Quarries
Stonework – Laings Stone Masons
Metalwork (corona) – Dearnside Fabricators Ltd.**

A crucial factor in the whole design process was the combining of two uses into one cohesive and workable whole. Particular consideration from day one focused on the siting of the auditorium, which would be at the heart of the development.

BBC BUILDING /
LEEDS COLLEGE OF MUSIC
DLA ARCHITECTURE LIMITED

Quarry Hill, Leeds

Construction Value: £6.5 million
Completion Date: 2003

Description

The building provides 1,850 m^2 of office space and studios for the BBC, and a 360-seat auditorium for Leeds College of Music.

History

The site was one of the key 'gateways' identified in the Terry Farrell masterplan for the Quarry Hill area, which was commissioned by Leeds City Council. In a prominent position within that key development area, the extremely constrained site was formerly home to an open-air car park.

Client's Brief

The brief stipulated a design that successfully combined the specialist needs of both the BBC and the expanding Leeds College of Music within one single building envelope. The site was deliberately chosen as it sat within the rapidly developing cultural quarter of Leeds.

Design Process

A crucial factor in the whole design process was the combining of two uses into one cohesive and workable whole. Particular consideration from day one focused on the siting of the auditorium, which would be at the heart of the development. Understandably, initial proposals placed it at the base of the scheme – forming a central core, around which the BBC facilities could be stacked. As the design process evolved, careful consideration was given to the movement of people throughout the building and, due to the sharing of facilities, it was found possible to elevate the auditorium to the top of the building. Walkways and bridges were suggested to link with the college's existing stairways and lifts, which would provide access to the rooftop facilities. These links also enabled the creation of spill-out space and bar areas for use during performances.

Alterations to the location of the auditorium also helped to effectively fulfil the BBC's '20-20 Vision' – to bring

DLA ARCHITECTURE LTD

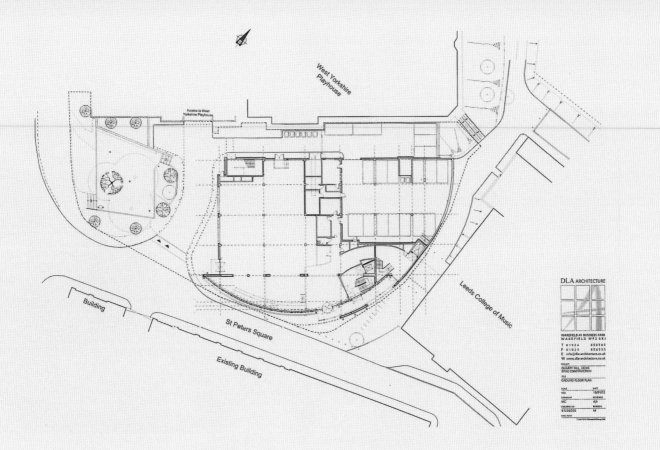

St Peters Square

Existing Building

Building

West Yorkshire Playhouse

Access to West Yorkshire Playhouse

Leeds College of Music

DLA ARCHITECTURE

WAKEFIELD 41 BUSINESS PARK
WAKEFIELD WF2 0XJ
T 01924 850965
F 01924 850555
E info@dla-architecture.co.uk
W www.dla-architecture.co.uk
PROJECT
QUARRY HILL, LEEDS
STAGE CONSTRUCTION
TITLE
GROUND FLOOR PLAN
SCALE   DATE
NTS   16/01/02
DRAWN BY   REVIEWED
MC   djb
DRAWING NO   REVISION
97236/200   M
DWG PATH

broadcasting more in touch with the general public. With the use of extensive glazing at low level, an openness and welcoming feel to the BBC's entrance on the ground floor was achieved. Architecturally, this worked particularly well when applied in contrast to the solidity and curved form of the college's facilities. The choice of materials also complemented the simple shapes and design of the auditorium and back-of-house spaces.

When it came to construction, acoustic separation was the key determinant. Noise transfer had to be eliminated – in effect, the designers had to ensure that at any time a full orchestra could be playing in the auditorium whilst someone was reading the news in a studio below. Hence, a double structure was needed – creating the two independent levels of the building.

As part of an emerging cultural quarter and as one of only a small number of new civic buildings in Leeds' city centre, the building envelope itself needed to be architecturally strong. A considered approach to design, careful choice of materials and appreciation of client needs allowed the architects to create a legible scheme that combines both the building's uses and enhances the overall architectural diversity of the city.

Project Sign-off

As part of this emerging quarter of Leeds, the building makes a positive contribution to the city skyline. In particular, its prominence and presence as a civic building elevates its stature within the city's architectural mix. Not only does it enhance the architectural amenity of the central area, but associated public-realm work – and particularly the installation of high-quality public art in the adjacent St Peter's Square – adds to the overall social value of the scheme. In addition, it is important to remember that these facilities provide a high-quality performance venue that promotes the city of Leeds and attracts visitors to it.

WWW.JH-JPHOTO.CO.UK

PROJECT TEAM

Client/Building Owner: **Rushbond plc**
Architect: **DLA Architecture Limited**
Quantity Surveyor: **Turner Townsend**
Structural Engineer: **Building Design Partnership**
Main Contractor: **Birse**

73

The overall built element is conceived as a landscape form, occupying a prominent location on the valley ridge running through the city centre. The proposal draws on references to the region's geological forms and to Yorkshire's rich sculptural heritage.

BROADCASTING PLACE

FEILDEN CLEGG BRADLEY STUDIOS

Woodhouse Lane, Leeds

Construction Value: Estimated £30 million
Completion Date: Summer 2009

Description

Broadcasting Place combines the new Faculty of Arts & Society for Leeds Metropolitan University (Leeds Met) with student accommodation and a new Baptist church.

History

The site was home to the BBC Radio & Television Studios, which recently moved eastwards to new headquarters at Quarry Hill. It contains the listed structures of the former Broadcasting House Building and a former Baptist church, currently the regional headquarters of Unison, both of which are retained in the proposed scheme. It is bounded by roads to all sides – most prominently to the south, where the city's inner ring road is located in an open cutting.

Client's Brief

Downing Developments' brief was to create a new academic facility capable of accommodating the Leeds Met Faculty of Arts & Society. A new home for the Blenheim Baptist Church was also required, to replace the existing 1950s building. The brief additionally asked for 240 student rooms in residential 'clusters' and studios, with associated ancillary and management facilities.

Design Process

The Broadcasting Place site had a previous planning approval for a scheme comprising a series of small-floorplate buildings which provided student residential accommodation. Feilden Clegg Bradley Studios were appointed to bring forward a revised scheme that created a new academic facility for Leeds Met in combination with student housing and a new Blenheim Baptist Church. Key principles for the development of the site had been established for the previous proposal, in dialogue with the Civic Architect and the city's planning department. These principles included a

significant pedestrian route through the site, the creation of a new courtyard space, a respect for the scale and grain of surrounding listed buildings, the location of taller buildings towards a 'gateway' location into the city centre and a simple palette of natural materials.

The design approach focused on the new pedestrian route, which naturally divided the building into two principal forms around a central court. The lower-rise element addresses the scale of the two adjacent listed buildings and forms the main entrance elevation onto Woodhouse Lane. The higher building screens the heart of the site from the busy Blenheim Way, while rising to a 23-storey tower which looks back towards the city centre. The low-rise block houses lecture rooms, administrative facilities and teaching spaces for the faculty, all around a covered court. The higher-rise building houses workshops and open-plan studio spaces for the architecture, landscape design, graphics and fine art departments, with the tower accommodating the student residential accommodation.

The overall built element is conceived as a landscape form, occupying a prominent location on the valley ridge running through the city centre. The proposal draws on references to the region's geological forms and to Yorkshire's rich sculptural heritage. The two buildings have strongly raking roofs, which rise to follow the topography of the valley ridge and which allow them to mediate between the low-rise listed buildings and the skyline tower. The treatment of the elevations follows on from this attitude to landscape, with openings treated as water passing through rock formations. This aesthetic is reinforced by the use of two simple materials: a corten steel cladding punctuated by glazing in the form either of windows or of curtain walling. However, the configuration of the elevations was not only considered aesthetically; an extensive analysis was also undertaken

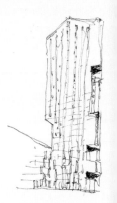

FEILDEN CLEGG BRADLEY STUDIOS

FEILDEN CLEGG BRADLEY STUDIOS

FEILDEN CLEGG BRADLEY STUDIOS

FEILDEN CLEGG BRADLEY STUDIOS

by the Building Research Establishment (BRE) to map daylighting requirements across all façades of the new buildings.

Project Sign-off

The project has commenced on site and is due for completion during the summer of 2009.

PROJECT TEAM

Client/Building Owner: **Downing Developments (GMD)**

Architect: **Feilden Clegg Bradley Studios**

Quantity Surveyor: **Walfords**

Structural Engineer: **Halcrow Yolles**

Services Engineer: **KGA Partnership**

Main Contractor: **George Downing Construction**

Fire Consultant: **Warrington Fire Research Consultancy**

75

In City Square the impact of the building is key, and it balances the Post Office and Queen's Hotel on the other sides of the square.

NO. 1 CITY SQUARE

AEDAS ARCHITECTS LIMITED

No. 1 City Square, Leeds

Construction Value: £14 million
Completion Date: June 1994

Description

A new-build office complex on the site of a previous 1960s building, No. 1 City Square was one of the first commercial developments to eschew the then prevalent 'Leeds Look'.

History

Restrictions arising from the previous building were fundamental, and the closure and removal of a high-level walkway was prioritised. This permitted redevelopment, with a scheme designed to address the city and to be focused towards City Square. Essential to the urban setting of the scheme, this allowed the present building form to enclose City Square and define entry points to Park Row and Infirmary Street, where previously the boundaries of the square had been unclear.

Client's Brief

Following a review of earlier feasibility schemes, the client's brief was defined as the creation of good naturally daylit office space with a column-free floorplate, whilst optimising the developable area of the site.

Design Process

In its contribution to Leeds, the building's design was considered to have both citywide and City Square-focused criteria. In townscape terms, the contribution to the Leeds skyline of buildings at the heart of its commercial core was important, and No. 1's urban setting amongst familiar landmarks influenced the form of the fabric roof and its night-time illumination. In City Square the impact of the building is key, and it balances the Post Office and Queen's Hotel on the other sides of the square. Again, the impact and expression of the building by night was considered at an early stage. In elevation, the selection of materials and treatment of the façades responds appropriately to the established solid-and-void pattern of the buildings in neighbouring

Infirmary Street and Park Row. As traditional banking streets, the permanence and security expressed by this treatment is repeated in the fenestration pattern of the limestone-based reconstructed stone cladding. The form of the building comprises two blocks with a 'cleft' of glass linking the solid forms of Park Row and Wine Street. Where these blocks are bridged by office space, it is fully glazed on all north- and south-facing walls to achieve the transparency of the central space. This glazed element also expresses all horizontal and vertical movement within the building, adding interest and movement to the façade and the urban square.

The central atrium is a stable environment, conditioned by extract air from the office floors and uniformly lit through its northern glazed wall. Glazing was considered for the roof, but would have had inherent self-weight, solar-gain and glare problems. The lightweight Teflon fabric allowed its supporting structure to be more elegant, avoided glare problems owing to its opacity, and achieved the sought-after skyline contribution by both day and night. To punctuate the uniform lighting, each cone-shaped element of the roof is joined by clear inflated ETFE cushions, and this material also seals the 'live' roof to the solid building and accommodates differential movement. The clear band between the cladding and fabric roof allows the latter to 'float' over the atrium and project forward into City Square in order to protect the entrance podium space.

Project Sign-off

The design of this dramatic office building marked a change in the architecture of Leeds city centre. It successfully challenged planning restrictions on height in order to achieve a statement worthy of its position on the northern side of City Square – a location that constitutes many people's first impression of the centre upon arrival. The accompanying sculpture, of birds flying up the side of the building in circular formation, adds to the attraction.

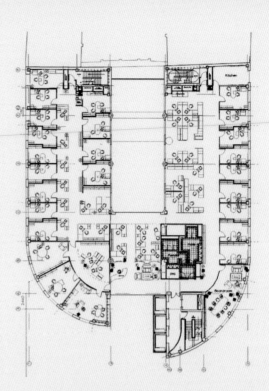

ALL IMAGES ON THIS SPREAD ARE COURTESY OF AEDAS ARCHITECTS LIMITED

PROJECT TEAM

Client/Building Owner: **Norwich Union Investment Management**

Architect: **Aedas Architects Limited**

Quantity Surveyor: **Davis Langdon & Everest**

Structural Engineer: **Deakin Callard & Partners**

Services Engineer: **Furness Green Partnership**

Main Contractor: **Shepherd Construction**

Leeds City Council wished to
celebrate the centenary of the
square in 2003 by undertaking a
full restoration project.

CITY SQUARE
LEEDS CITY COUNCIL

Junction of Park Row and Boar Lane, Leeds

Construction Value: £2.5 million
Completion Date: 2003

Description

The re-creation of the historic element of a large
triangular space at the centre of the city including the
re-grouping of 13 listed Edwardian statues.

History

The space was created between 1893 and 1903 to
celebrate the grant of City status to the former Borough.
A new General Post Office building was sited to form a
new triangular space following demolition of an 18th-
century Cloth Hall. The formal Edwardian layout was
totally modified by a 1960s traffic scheme.

Client's Brief

Leeds City Council wished to celebrate the centenary
of the square in 2003 by undertaking a full restoration
project.

The key elements of the brief were:

- to restore the central part of the square to
  reflect its original circular geometry

- to regroup the 13 listed bronze statues in a formal
  arrangement – inspired by the Edwardian layout

- to work in the context of the re-aligned traffic
  arrangement designed to accommodate a 'supertram' station on the east side of the square

- to introduce trees, seating and a water
  feature into the scheme.

Other details of the brief included the continuity of the
tradition of placing the city's major Christmas tree within
the space, the exploration of the possibility of closing
the highway on the northwest side of the space and
incorporating it into the pedestrian scheme and the
inclusion of a defined cycle route across the square.

Materials and detailing were to be of the highest quality,
sustainable lighting to be created and the new layout to

be related to the symmetry of the Post Office building.

Design Process

The design process began with historical research
– through documentary, map progression and
photographic evidence – into the evolution of the space.
Its medieval origins lay in the fields of the manorial park
which started here on the western boundary of the town
which was established by charter in 1207.

In the 18th and early 19th centuries a large new Cloth
Hall, a General Infirmary, a Unitarian Chapel and a Court
House were built at the junction of two principal streets
– historic Boar Lane and the new Park Row. The latter
street was created to commence a Georgian west-end
development of the town. The mid and late 19th century
brought three adjacent railway stations and the attached
Queen's Hotel. Following the demolition of the Cloth Hall,
a combined central Post Office and Telegraph Office
was built. These new technologies of railway travel
and international telegraph communications made City
Square the new focus of the city. A Leeds industrialist
and medievalist, Colonel Harding, recommended and
substantially funded the creation of the new space.
He conceived a circular, granite-balustraded central
space with a majestic equestrian figure by Brock at its
centre. This was the reflection of his medieval interests,
celebrating – with no apparent relevance to Leeds – the
victory of the Black Prince at Crécy on 26 August 1346.

The former entries to the central circle had pairs of
nymphs representing Night and Morn. This symbolist
sculpture was by Drury – avant-garde and rare in public
art in 1903.

Finally, four bronze statues of figures associated with
the city or industrial invention were aligned – modestly
leading to their backs being turned to the nymphs.
These were of Watt (steam power), Priestley (minister of

78

Mill Hill Chapel and chemist), Harrison (17th-century philanthropist) and Hook (Vicar of Leeds and social ecclesiologist of the mid-19th century).

Public toilets were placed beneath the square. Trams arrived in the early 20th century and traffic in the mid-20th century, both of which pressurised the Square's original formality which was finally lost in the highway scheme of the1960s.

The design process, through sketches and wide consultations, led to agreement on the closure of the road fronting the Post Office so as to produce a new, calm place in busy City Square. A semi-circular layout – based on the Post Office's symmetry and the fixed point of the Black Prince – echoed the lost circular symmetry of the Edwardian scheme. The full circular layout could not be re-created due to the established 'loop traffic' route and the layout proposed to accommodate the tram. Once this semi-circular idea was established – and, crucially, original Aberdeen granite balusters were discovered by timely chance – the granite and sandstone paving pattern and balustrade layout was drawn. Seating, water jets, filigree 'gleditsia'

trees, lighting columns, statues and a Christmas tree socket were all arranged in semi-circular symmetry. Stainless steel and bronze were used for seats, litter bins and lighting columns. The hydraulics for the fountain jets were housed within perimeter grey granite walls. A cycle route follows the outer rim of the semi-circular layout.

As an example of public realm energising perimeter uses, restaurants and serviced apartments now occupy the restored former Post Office – with tables set out within the new space. The space was duly opened in celebration of the city's centenary – and included the participation of Martin Wainwright and his family. Martin's great-grandfather, in funding the statue of Watt, was one of two Leeds figures who responded to Colonel Harding's appeal for civic-minded support for his great scheme.

During the past decade, new or refurbished buildings have formed a positive background to the space. In a clockwise circuit from the conversion of the Post Office, No. 1 City Square has echoed in its semi-circular frontage the Edwardian building on that site demolished in the 1960s. No. 1 Park Row forms the northwest

corner of the Square, the 19th century Mill Hill Chapel on the east side was cleaned and restored, a 1960s corner tower block was re-clad in silver panels and made into a hotel, whilst the domed former Yorkshire Bank and 1930s Queens Hotel form the southern edges of the Square. The 1921 Majestic cinema was restored in its transformation into a night club.

The project in effect put the heart back into the Square whilst traffic to the southern edge and a 'tram station' on its eastern side remain as unresolved elements of the space. These are currently under creative review.

Project sign-off

The 'centenary' project for City Square has become a rich amalgam of the revived formality of an Edwardian civic space and the vitality of outdoor restaurant life, pedestrian movement, fountain jets, trees, planting and seating. It has established a momentum for the resolution of the traffic and transportation pressures which affect other parts of the square.

PROJECT TEAM

Client/Building Owner: **Leeds City Council**

Architect: **Leeds Civic Architect**

Engineer: **Highways, public space, services and costings: Leeds City Council Highways Engineers**

Main Contractor: **Wrekin**

At the Henry Moore Institute, the existing four-storey buildings naturally divide vertically to give galleries at upper ground floor served by storage and plant rooms at lower ground floor.

HENRY MOORE INSTITUTE

DIXON JONES

Victoria Square, Leeds

Construction Value: £4 million
Completion Date: February 1994

Description

A new home for Leeds' collection of 'local boy' Henry Moore's sculptures, in a conversion of existing domestic-scale properties located in a prominent position on the city's main thoroughfare, the Headrow. The Institute was a fine early example of the non-'Leeds Look'.

History

The Institute occupies three converted 19th-century wool merchants' offices at the end of Cookridge Street. These existing buildings are domestic in character, with significant elevations to Cookridge and Alexander Streets. The conversion had to strike a balance between the retention of the existing structure and the particular needs of a sculpture institute.

Design Process

In the design of a project one has to keep a look out for useful accident; and perhaps there is a state of mind worth cultivating that allows the thought process to be deflected when an interesting accident appears. At the Henry Moore Institute, the main entrance leads to the far end of the plan before turning through a hairpin bend back on itself to enter the new daylit main gallery. Progressing from the entrance deeper into the plan, the light level drops and the pupils of visitors' eyes naturally dilate. Turning 180° to face the bright gallery hugely dramatises the impact of encountering raw daylight. This is the most unexpected moment in the building — even though the visual effect was completely unpredicted.

A chance visit to an exhibition of Minimalist artists and sculptors at the Liverpool Tate in 1988 had a profound effect on Dixon Jones ideas for the Institute. After many years of wrestling with the repair of cities and the visual complexities of their Royal Opera House project, the work of the Minimalists came as a breath of fresh air. It jogged the memory that the reductive layouts of

their early Runcorn and Milton Keynes housing projects had displayed many of the identifying characteristics of Minimalism. This was confirmed by a chance discovery of a series of 1972 Richard Serra sculptures identical to the 'simultaneous sculpture' proposition for the Netherfield housing in Milton Keynes.

At the Henry Moore Institute, the existing four-storey buildings naturally divide vertically to give galleries at upper ground floor served by storage and plant rooms at lower ground floor. This leaves the first floor as a study centre and the second floor for administration. The only new building is the main gallery space, created by filling in the existing courtyard to Alexander Street. A bridge links the existing Leeds City Art Gallery to the new Institute at first-floor level.

The sculpture galleries are simple, white spaces with a minimum of detail. Their character comes from the quality of daylight and the contrasting scales of the spaces available within the existing structures. The study centre and the administration level are detailed in a different manner from the galleries, using natural oak in order to give a relaxed environment in which to work.

To understand the approach to the design of the exterior of the project, one has to look at the recent history of this area of Leeds. The square started as a much smaller public space in front of the Town Hall. Subsequently, this space was enlarged by removing a block of city buildings and by shortening Cookridge Street. As a result, a number of public buildings now line the square that were never intended to face in that direction. Although the City Art Gallery had already had a new façade added in 1976 to relate it properly to the Headrow, the exposed end elevation of the last three properties in Cookridge Street (which now house the Henry Moore Institute) had been left as a raw unresolved

STUDY OF SCULPTURE
TOILETS

83

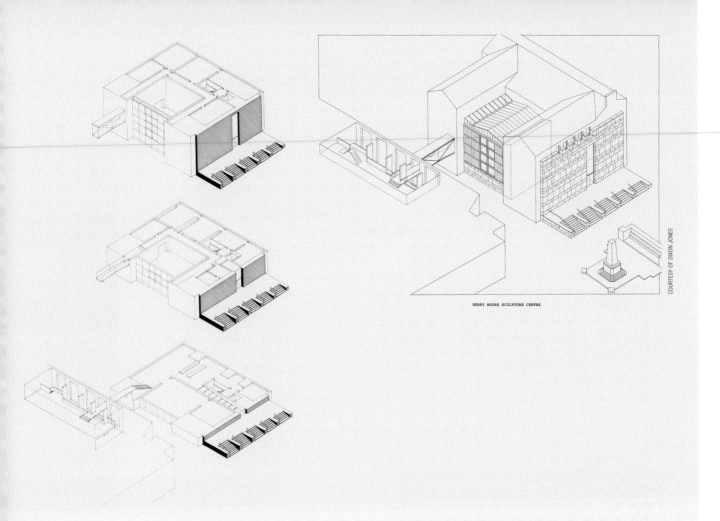

HENRY MOORE SCULPTURE CENTRE

party wall facing the main square of Leeds. There was therefore a special responsibility to complete the series of new façades to the Headrow by making an appropriate main entrance to the new Institute.

This new entrance takes the form of a minimalist sculptural idea, using the mechanical repetition of flights of steps generated as the ground falls across the frontage. The entrance doors are located in a stone wall placed against the end of the terrace so as to leave explicit the 'cut' made through Cookridge Street in order to create the enlarged Headrow. The whole entrance structure is made of granite used in its various natural forms. The vertical surfaces are all polished and the horizontal surfaces are all 'flamed' to give a contrasting rough texture. A tall, eccentrically placed slot in the polished wall marks the entrance, behind which is the shallow stepped passage that leads to the galleries.

Whereas the elevation to the Headrow expresses permanence, the elevation to the gallery filling in the courtyard is intended to look less permanent than the surrounding brick structures. It consists of a grid of bronze frames filled with natural oak and obscure glass, and it incorporates a pair of giant doors to give access for large sculptures.

Project Sign-off

The building was commissioned in 1990, and the building contract lasted from January 1992 until completion in February 1994.

The Henry Moore Institute won the 1993 RIBA Award, and a Civic Trust Award in the same year.

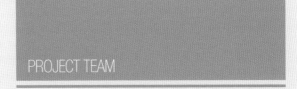

PROJECT TEAM

Client/Building Owner: **Leeds City Art Gallery**
Architect: **Dixon Jones**
Quantity Surveyor: **Stern and Woodford**
Structural Engineer: **Alan Baxter & Associates**
Services Engineer: **BDP Services**
Main Contractor: **Mowlem Management Limited**

85

The architects envisaged a tall building that would connect the teaching accommodation into the existing circulation, with cluster-flats, each with six student rooms, above.

LEEDS COLLEGE OF MUSIC

ALLEN TOD ARCHITECTURE LIMITED

3 Quarry Hill, Leeds

Construction Value: £7 million
Completion Date: September 2005

Description

A new-build project, comprising 200 units of student accommodation situated above new college facilities.

History

The development intensifies the use of a plot that had contained a car park and a substation for the college, and which was, in effect, a contaminated, brownfield site.

Client's Brief

Demand was for teaching space and some student accommodation to match the college's success and its need to respond to the changing context of Higher Education. The architects envisaged a tall building that would connect the teaching accommodation into the existing circulation, with cluster-flats, each with six student rooms, above.

Design Process

Overlaying the rigours of student accommodation and college facilities the design explores the phenomenon of synaesthesia, where people's senses are scrambled so that, for instance, 'Thursday' is perceived as 'blue', 'middle C' is 'green', 'yellow' is 'sour', etc. The most common form of this condition is a mix between music and colour, and many artists/musicians have played with this combination. The façades are therefore conceived as a musical score.

In terms of the built project, the desired overall effect is to break the repetitive form of student housing into a rich pattern of reflecting surfaces that fragments or dissolves the mass of the building, changing its appearance with the time of day and lighting conditions so that it retains some surprises. The form is simplified into three 'boxes' – a plinth, which ties the extension to the original building; the main body of the building, with

the design wrapped around all sides; and a lightbox to cap off the composition at the top.

The city planning officers were initially wary of a tall building on the site. Allen Tod Architecture, however, developed a series of bold elevational treatments that were intended to create an iconic building whilst increasing the capacity of the site to three floors of teaching accommodation and up to 11 storeys of student rooms. The final multicoloured pixellated design caught the planners' imagination, and, once the height was agreed using 3-D modelling studies of Quarry Hill, they championed the scheme.

The building used a steel frame for speed of construction, concrete decks and relatively inexpensive stock materials: blue brick and coloured spandrel glass. The teaching spaces were completed to shell standard, and the flats finished to the specification of national student-accommodation provider, Unite.

A repetitive, relatively inexpensive form of development, this student housing block nonetheless makes a powerful, yet subtle, intervention into the skyline of Leeds. The architects' solution reduces the complexity of the form, and by using standard glass products lifts the quality of the building. The use of glass will ensure that the colours and finish will remain over the life of the building. The design brings great benefits to the College of Music and its students, by allowing the development of a tiny site in an effective and intense way.

The concept design options were appraised in May 2001, and the subsequent planning submission made in February 2003. Completion was achieved in September 2005.

The main architectural ambition of this project has been to contribute to the skyline of the city, where there is a new 'Leeds Look' emerging. The increase in the scale of recent new development has brought with it elevations that aim to break up the mass of these proposals with collages of cladding materials. Allen Tod Architecture's elevations for this project demonstrate a clear and simple form, which relies on materials whose look changes with the weather. Since the building was completed, it has become clear that its appearance does in fact alter throughout the day and that its form is animated by pattern and light.

The completed project is an example of bold and challenging architecture emerging from an ordinary building type. It shows that an architecture which is uncompromising yet subtle can make a distinctive impression on the city.

The project was delivered as a PF1 type development partnership with a team led by Totty Construction with Robinson Architects.

PROJECT TEAM

Client/Building Owner: **Leeds College of Music**
Architect: **Allen Tod Architecture Limited**
Quantity Surveyor: **RBA**
Main Contractor: **Totty Construction with Robinson Architects**

The existing listed building fronting Boar Lane had an attractive stone façade, which expressed the commercial success of Victorian Leeds.

TREVELYAN SQUARE

CHAPMAN TAYLOR

Boar Lane, Leeds

Construction Value: £12 million
Completion Date: 1991

Description

Two buildings enclosing a new public square: a large T-shaped block to the rear (south) of the site, and a smaller block incorporating an existing listed frontage onto Boar Lane.

History

Trevelyan Square is a new urban space enclosed by four buildings. The two buildings to the north and south of the square, and the square itself, were designed by Chapman Taylor; the 250-bed hotel to the east and the offices and 650-space car park to the west were by others.

The listed buildings fronting onto Boar Lane were designed by Thomas Ambler (1838–1920).

Client's Brief

The client required an office development on this prime city-centre plot adjoining the railway station. The site had been a surface car park resulting from bomb damage during the Second World War. There were, however, substantial remains of an attractive Victorian building fronting onto Boar Lane, whilst the rear of the site is bordered by a railway viaduct.

Design Process

Some time was spent in designing a large retail scheme on the site, with connections across Boar Lane to the existing Bond Street and Trinity Shopping Centres. However, difficulties of land ownership and connectivity through the site – the latter owing to the need to retain the listed building fronting Boar Lane – together with rising development costs and a decline, at that time, in the retail market, rendered these schemes unviable. The brief subsequently switched to mixed-use development in a piecemeal fashion, with commercial offices as the dominant element. Chapman Taylor recognised that the edges of the site constituted a somewhat hostile

environment, owing to heavy traffic on Boar Lane and a noisy and rather unsightly railway viaduct along the southern boundary, and they therefore decided to group the buildings around a new urban square. The square functioned in two ways: partly to offer an attractive outlook for all the buildings facing onto it, but also to provide a suitable entrance setting which effectively extended the commercial frontage of Boar Lane into a backland site.

The existing listed building fronting Boar Lane had an attractive stone façade, which expressed the commercial success of Victorian Leeds. The architects thought that it should be restored and that the new buildings should respect the style, quality and materials of that period. To that end they felt it important that the detailing of these buildings should incorporate a feeling of solidarity with the older structure, and this feeling is emphasised by their use of deep window reveals, strong cornices and heavy copings.

The rear building was designed in a T shape to provide two small but carefully landscaped private courtyard gardens which give a calm and pleasant outlook for the office workers in contrast to the setting of the railway viaduct. It contains 2,000 m² of commercial space, while the smaller building fronting onto Boar Lane contains 7,000 m² of offices above ground-level retail units.

The central square includes a stone fountain which the architects found in an architectural salvage yard. It provides a focal point and gives character and identity to the urban square in which it sits.

PROJECT TEAM

Client/Building Owner: **MEPC**
Current Building Owner: **Standard Life Investment Fund**
Architect: **Chapman Taylor**
Quantity Surveyor: **Mark Dunstone Associates**
Structural Engineer: **Ove Arup & Partners**
Services Engineer: **BSC Consulting Engineers**
Main Contractor: **Higgs & Hill**

Whitehall Waterfront was the first
building to be delivered as part of a very
high-profile masterplan to extend the city
centre west along the River Aire.

WHITEHALL WATERFRONT

CAREYJONES ARCHITECTS

Whitehall Road, 2 Riverside Way, Leeds

Construction Value: £42 million
Completion Date: Summer 2004

Description

This centrally located riverside scheme contains 193 contemporary apartments with undercroft car parking.

The 1,250 m^2 ground-floor space comprises a mix of office and bar/restaurant accommodation, and there is also a 600 m^2 penthouse office suite.

History

The riverside frontage of the site, along Whitehall Road, was for many years home to a soap factory, known locally as 'Soapy Joe's', latterly owned by Lever Brothers who manufactured shampoo on the site up until the early 1980s. Following its purchase by Town Centre Securities, the plot was cleared and utilised for a time as a surface car park.

Client's Brief

The site was purchased with an Outline Approval set within a much broader masterplan, which effectively established its massing, footprint and use-class principles. A predominantly residential developer, the client wanted a building with apartments that would be attractive to the investor market and private purchaser alike. The design was to incorporate a parking ratio approaching 70 per cent of the apartment numbers, with active frontage to the lower floors.

Design Process

Following the criteria established within the outline consent, careyjones architects sought to create a dynamic building form that would take maximum advantage of its location against the riverside and its south-facing amenity, with uninterrupted views across Leeds city centre as well as beyond in all directions. The site also lies a short walk from the railway station, main shopping centre and business quarter.

Whitehall Waterfront was the first building to be delivered as part of a very high-profile masterplan to extend the city centre west along the River Aire, which, when complete, will provide 46,000 m^2 of office accommodation, 400 residential units, 3,000 m^2 of retail and restaurant space and a 500-space multi-storey car park.

The given massing and footprint of the scheme had been designed to form a 'bookend' to the complete riverside elevation – with this particular building sitting at a near 90-degree bend of the River Aire, rising to 14 storeys and then dropping to ten. Integral to the design concept was the open space addressing the riverside itself. Facing directly south, bar and restaurant uses at ground-floor level here could benefit greatly from an environment that encouraged Continental-style dining.

The elevations were designed to break down the large mass of the building to an appropriate scale, by using a layering of materials. As a whole, the intention was to create a deliberate plinth at the bottom two floor levels, in order to 'ground' the building form, and to cap the upper levels with a feature of a much lighter glazed appearance, leaving a central band with a more regular fenestration pattern.

Constructed with a steel frame and pre-cast concrete floor planks, the finished building sits above two levels of basement car park whose design required careful consideration owing to the proximity of the river. Driven sheet-steel piling, with all joints fully welded, was used once the ground had been removed, in order to ensure the longevity of the basement construction.

© CHRIS GASCOIGNE/VIEW

CAREYJONES ARCHITECTS

Project Sign-off

This area of development land is unique in Leeds, owing to its size and location – lying close to the city centre and railway station, and being south facing with river frontage.

Whitehall Waterfront has been the catalyst for the entire development, positioned at the far end of the site to allow for progressive phases to 'close the gap' on the city centre. It has set out to establish a standard to which all future phases will aspire, maintaining and embracing a truly mixed-use regeneration project within one of the UK's fastest-growing cities.

PROJECT TEAM

Client/Building Owner: **Town Centre Securities**
Architect: **careyjones architects**
Quantity Surveyor: **AYH**
Structural Engineer: **Deakin Walton**
Services Engineer: **Silcock Dawson**
Main Contractor: **HBG**

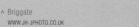

^ Briggate
WWW.JH-JPHOTO.CO.UK

^ Alley off Lands Lane
WWW.JH-JPHOTO.CO.UK

^ The City Palace of Varieties music hall
© IAN GRUNDY

CONNECTED LEEDS

When Nolli drew his famous plan of Rome in 1748, he showed as open space all the public places of the city, streets and piazze, palazzo courtyards and church interiors – in fact, anywhere where the native Roman or visitor on the Grand Tour could wander. It is just such a blend of accessible spaces which makes up Connected Leeds: sometimes inside, sometimes outside; sometimes covered, sometimes open.

By excluding the traffic from the smaller streets of the city centre between Park Row and Briggate one of Britain's biggest pedestrian areas has been created, centred on Albion Place and Lands Lane, which returns the streets to the people. On one little alley off Lands Lane can be found the City Palace of Varieties, its multi-galleried c.1850 auditorium a last remaining memory of the music-hall tradition. Also off Lands Lane runs Thornton's Arcade, Early English Gothic Revival of 1878 with a pointed glass vault, while, on the far side of Briggate, is the County Arcade, all terracotta and tinsel and built 20 years later. Taller, grander and designed by one of the best Edwardian theatre architects, Frank Matcham, its cruciform plan suggests the great arcades of fin de siècle Europe. Through the County Arcade lies Vicar Lane, with the reconditioned

^ Thornton's Arcade
WWW.JH-JPHOTO.CO.UK

^ County Arcade
WWW.JH-JPHOTO.CO.UK

> City Markets
WWW.JH-JPHOTO.CO.UK

> Corn Exchange roof
WWW.JH-JPHOTO.CO.UK

95

ᴧᴧ The Dark Arches
WWW.JH-JPHOTO.CO.UK

ᴧ Station main foyer
WWW.JH-JPHOTO.CO.UK

City Markets and the Corn Exchange towards its end. Both are galleried, public spaces covered by expressive roof structures: the one, cast iron and complex; the other, timber and elegantly simple.

Connected Leeds is also the Calls, where the reconditioned warehouses and the Centenary Bridge have brought new life to the waterfront. Along these waterways, the River Aire and the adjacent Leeds and Liverpool Canal cut between 1770 and 1816, and on the railways high above, industrial Leeds connected with the Empire. Here the great engineer John Rennie started building the Wellington Bridge, an elliptical arch of 30 m span, two years after the battle of Waterloo. The equally commemorative Victoria Bridge, designed by George Leather and erected in 1837, celebrated that queen's accession to the throne. The layers of public space which make up Leeds Railway Station, from the

quays and mighty brick vaults below to the spacious concourse behind William Curtis Green's elegantly stripped Queen's Hotel of 1934, contrast with the bulky tubular steel frame, neither mighty nor elegant, within the recently rebuilt station shed. Nevertheless, a good view of Holbeck and Armley, as well as a cup of coffee, can be obtained from the bridge beneath the canopy which takes passengers over the tracks.

Connected Leeds is a Leeds through which one can wander. Like other cold, northern cities – Montreal, perhaps, or Prague – its arcades and galleries allow one to escape the weather, but like Nolli's Rome it is a series of warm, sunlit spaces for those moments that cannot be missed.

The client required a spatial and building-
development framework with clearly defined
streets and urban edges – its gradual
development to proceed around a sequence
of clearly connected public spaces

WELLINGTON PLACE

CAREYJONES ARCHITECTS, FEILDEN CLEGG BRADLEY STUDIOS AND MARTHA SCHWARTZ PARTNERS

The site is bounded by Wellington Street, Northern Street, Whitehall Road and the River Aire.

Construction Value: £400 million
Completion Date: Anticipated: 2020

Description

A long-term, phased redevelopment, with complementary provision of public realm, comprising a range of mixed-use buildings on a site that has been fully cleared except for a lifting tower (a masonry railway structure).

History

An extensive 1840s railway terminus with goods yard and sheds, the site had tracks that crossed the River Aire, Leeds and Liverpool Canal and earlier railway lines on an elegant viaduct system, which led to raised stations.

Apart from the listed lifting tower, the plot was cleared for an early 1980s retail park, which has since been demolished.

Client's Brief

The client required a spatial and building-development framework with clearly defined streets and urban edges – its gradual development to proceed around a sequence of clearly connected public spaces.

The brief also stipulated that building forms and spatial patterns were to achieve a coherent overall identity whilst allowing for adaptability in use and materiality over a 10-15-year development period.

Design Process

The developer was actively engaged in design sessions with a design team comprising one landscape and two architectural practices, with supporting technical disciplines.

The proposal needed to respond to the city council's wish to enhance connectivity to waterfront areas of diverse character – especially the naturalised River Aire banks to the west. The southern side of Whitehall Road was required to have a boulevard character, and links to the northern, gridded 18th-century street patterns

were also a priority. Accordingly, ideas were shaped through participation in design-and-planning workshops established by Leeds City Council, and via presentations and workshops with the Plans Panel of the council and a wide range of consultees.

Orientation, wind-flow and key views within and beyond the site were defined as critical factors. The carriage-lifting tower was to become the focus of a large public square. The listed viaduct fragment to the west, although outside the site ownership, was to be regarded as a generator and connector of public routes.

The resultant outline planning approval reflects a robust yet adaptable scheme, which will be physically mapped on the cleared site by the developer – with building footprints defined by crushed demolition rubble within a temporarily surfaced layout of streets and spaces. A site management-and-marketing suite and the 'Renaissance Leeds' City Workshop space – together known as 'Wellington Central' – have been created from former shipping containers adjacent to the tower.

All of this is a reflection of the developer's wish to give public access, for diverse activities and events, to this large city-centre site during Wellington Place's long period of evolution.

Three buildings have been developed to detail design stage. Two of the three buildings have been submitted for, and granted full planning permission, which will establish levels of quality and civic presence for the whole development. They will create the first stretch of boulevard, the riverbank green space, street edges and well-proportioned streets between the buildings.

This first group of buildings is to be clad in stonework, whilst glazing to windows and atria will be extended to raking roofs and terraces contained within their roof forms.

98

FCB STUDIOS

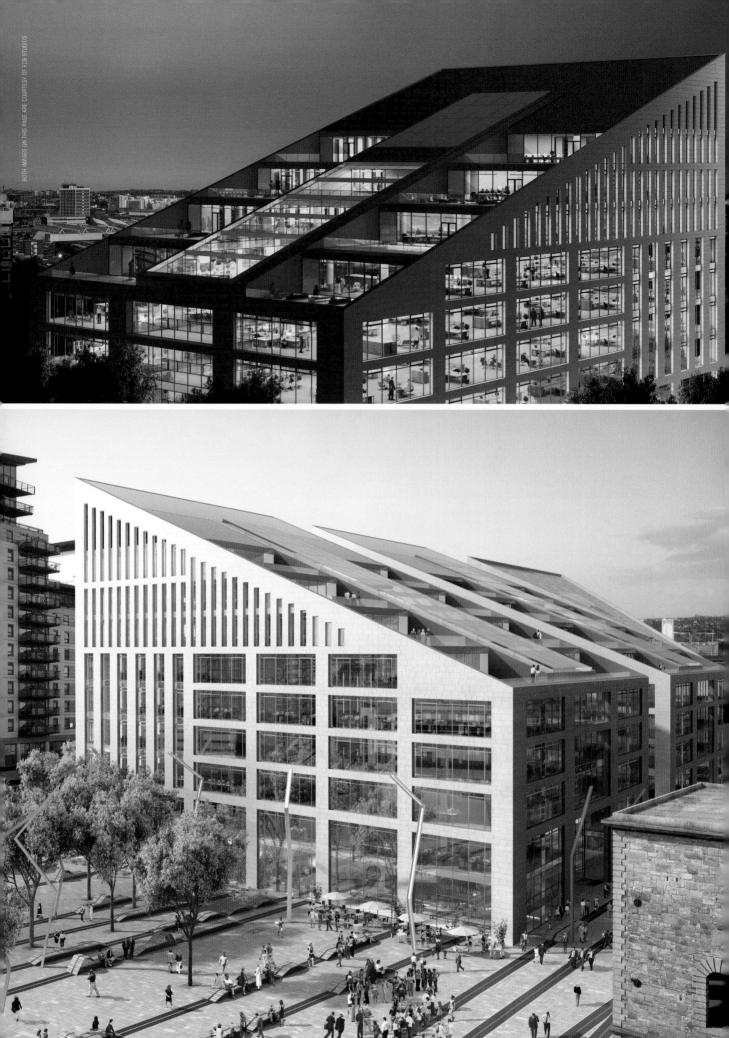

FCB STUDIOS AND CAREYJONES ARCHITECTS

The landscape character of the development adjusts according to context. On the banks of the River Aire, stepped terraces respond to flood-level predictions and produce a triangular space overall. Along the north side of Whitehall Road, a tree-lined avenue contains generous foot and cycle-ways.

At the heart of the project is another triangular space, focused on the historic lifting tower and similar in size to City Square. It will anchor this large development into the new 'West End' and draw together routes, connections and views across a wide area.

The constant theme underpinning the landscape proposals is the establishment of a colourful depiction of the remarkable pattern of railway lines which originally flowed at a high level above the site.

The longest route across the site will be defined by a canal-like 'cut', running from its northeast corner to the proposed access point onto the listed viaduct fragment, which crosses the river and canal.criterion, and the existing high-level overbridges, east and west of the station, proved to be integral to the design.

Project Sign-off

The whole project expresses a holistic approach to 'shaping the city', in which urban and landscape design is seen as a partnership activity. It also recognises that proposals need to respond to the evolution of the city over long periods of time.

This approach depends on the willingness of investor, developer, city council and design teams to commit to constant dialogue as use patterns and economic, technical and sustainability factors change or mature.

PROJECT TEAM

Wellington Place

Client: **MEPC**

Architect: **careyjones architects (Masterplanning Stage)**
Feilden Clegg Bradley Studios (Masterplanning Stage and Detailed Design Stage for first building group)

Landscape Architect: **Martha Schwartz Partners (Masterplanning Stage and Detailed Design Stage for first building group)**

Quantity Surveyor: **Davis Langdon**

Structural Engineer: **Arup**

Services Engineer: **Arup**

Main Contractor: **To be appointed**

Wellington Central
(incorporating the 'Renaissance Leeds' City Workshop)

Client/Building Owner: **MEPC**

Designer: **Martha Schwartz Partners**

Interiors (Marketing Suite): **Spatial Design Limited**

Workshop fit-out: **Oblong Furniture Limited**

Main Contractor: **Stonehouse Projects Limited**

101

A £245 million redevelopment of the complex was proposed, in order to increase track capacity and provide a station environment fit for the 21st century.

LEEDS CITY RAILWAY STATION
JEFFERSON SHEARD ARCHITECTS EGS

City Square, Leeds

Construction Value: £245 million
Completion Date: May 2002

Description

The design and construction of a covered railway station including track layout, signalling and overhead electrification. The project also provided new and extended platforms to cater for increased capacity.

History

The existing rail infrastructure of Leeds City Station was becoming increasingly unable to cater for its growing number of passengers and trains.

A £245 million redevelopment of the complex was therefore proposed, in order to increase track capacity and provide a station environment fit for the 21st century.

Client's Brief

The client required the poor existing station environment be improved by providing natural daylight and ventilation; improved passenger comfort and facilities, including information systems; and access for the mobility impaired.

Additional, and longer, platforms were also required, to ease train and passenger congestion. Most challenging of all, the construction was to be carried out without major disruption to the rail services.

Design Process

The railway passes through Leeds along an east–west axis and is carried on arches and bridges through the centre of the city, alongside the Conservation Areas of Holbeck, Granary Wharf, the River Aire and the Leeds and Liverpool Canal.

The new proposals utilised these arched structures to accommodate 'roof level foundations' and enclosures above.

Station Environment

The need to improve the environment by providing daylight penetration and natural ventilation was a major

COURTESY OF NETWORK RAIL AND JEFFERSON SHEARD ARCHITECTS

COURTESY OF NETWORK RAIL AND JEFFERSON SHEARD ARCHITECTS

intersecting roof profile with aluminium cladding, and the triangular trusses contain lighting, public-address and rainwater-disposal equipment, and are accessed via internal walkways in order to facilitate maintenance at high level, well away from the platform areas.

The sectional profile of the station building thus achieved improves and accelerates air flow, allowing exhaust fumes to vent out at high level. Glazed northlights, meanwhile, minimise solar heat gain and glare while providing consistent daylight levels.

A glazed façade on the western gable became the main passenger route to all through platforms from the overbridge. It also provides extensive views of the western approaches to Leeds, especially the Conservation Areas and canal basins.

Project Sign-off

The new Leeds Railway Station provides a modern rail interchange in the heart of the city. As the focus for a major regional transport hub, it will further enhance this vibrant city. It will also provide much-needed links to locations closer to home, such as the regenerated industrial village of Holbeck and other areas south of the River Aire.

COURTESY OF NETWORK RAIL AND JEFFERSON SHEARD ARCHITECTS

criterion, and the existing high-level overbridges, east and west of the station, proved to be integral to the design.

Options of over-cladding or alterations to the existing portal frame were discounted, as the roof had to be raised to improve environmental opportunities and accommodate the overbridges, thereby enabling them to be integrated into the development.

Early architectural concepts established a design philosophy of columns supporting long-span trusses and incorporating canted northlight glazing and horizontal ventilation apertures. Columns along the centrelines of the platforms provided wide open spaces at ground level, enabling easy passenger movement. Following this strategy, an excellent provision of natural light and ventilation was immediately achieved.

The curved form of the roof was primarily dictated by the railway's existing alignment, although it was raised to deliberately enhance the roof's distinct curvilinear appearance. The proposed tubular-steel roofing spars support a curved,

PROJECT TEAM

Client/Building Owner: **Network Rail (formerly Railtrack)**
Architect: **Jefferson Sheard EGS**
Structural Engineer: **Halcrow, White Young Green**
Main Contractor: **Birse, Wates**
Steelwork Fabricator: **Watson Steel Limited / Formscaff Limited**

The City Council worked in partnership with the developer to create a theatre for a diversity of groups from across the city to have performance, conference and educational facilities.

THE CARRIAGEWORKS
PANTHER HUDSPITH AND LEEDS CITY COUNCIL

Millennium Square, Leeds

Construction Value: £6 million
Completion Date: 2005

Description

A group of three connected buildings were restored and a new corner extension built. The buildings face two streets and also form two sides of Millennium Square.

History

The site lies within a Victorian street pattern with its northern edge created by demolition in the 1960s of swimming baths and back-to-back houses. Three attached buildings have distinctive character and originally served very different purposes: a printing works, a carriage manufactory, a corner shop and a Victorian office building.

Client's Brief

The City Council created a brief for a developer-led competition which had three aims – first, to restore and extend the listed buildings to form a key component of the new Millennium Square; second to ensure public access through the courtyard of the building group; and third to introduce a mix of uses which would complement and support the events activities on the Square. Design quality, use types and financial value of submissions were assessed and a scheme which included arts cinemas, office space and shops, bars and restaurants was selected.

Challenges in the provision of the arts cinemas led to the substitution of a new theatre project – this enabled the release of the existing Civic Theatre from the historic Leeds Institute and for the latter to become the new City Museum.

The City Council worked in partnership with the developer to create a theatre for a diversity of groups from across the city to have performance, conference and educational facilities.

Design Process

Leeds Civic Architect produced a conceptual scheme at the time of the competition to test and establish the feasibility of the building brief in the context of the planning and development brief for the site and to ensure that the criteria established for this component of the Millennium Square project were fulfilled.

A multi-disciplinary working group – including theatre and acoustic consultants – was set up by the council to work in close collaboration with the developer's professional and construction teams. A separate theatre fit-out briefing and design process was set up within the City Council.

The developer's architect, Panter Hudspith led the design of the shell works for the whole project with the Leeds Civic Architect's team as client architects for the City Council. A third team from the City's Design Services Agency led the theatre fit-out. Further design input came from the developer's tenants' fit-out requirements. This included a film and media studies department for Leeds Metropolitan University.

The finished building and spaces reflect the rich complexity of the briefing, design, restoration and construction processes.

A particular challenge in the project was to introduce a new 350-seat theatre structure with critical acoustic and fly-tower requirements into an historic building group of diverse character as well as form a strong corner presence on Millennium Square.

The theatre building stands on circular columns freeing lower levels for bar and restaurant uses, which spill out onto Millennium Square.

All the existing buildings proved adaptable for rehearsal rooms, storage and administration spaces for the theatre

use, for teaching spaces for Leeds Met and for bars, cafés and restaurant for diverse tenants.

The central courtyard of the building group had been given a glazed roof covering and stabilising of fabric had been undertaken as part of the Millennium Square project. This was taken forward by the developer's team to create public access to the complex as required by the brief.

Stone paving, under-floor heating, lighting and fabric restoration formed a space for all building users. Sheltered access to the theatre, spill-out seating from the bars and cafés and connectivity to streets and the adjacent Square and Mandela Garden have been created.

Choices of materials included a wide range of responses to historic materials in the building group - brick, stone, pine structural members, cast iron restoration, metal casements, timber sash windows, slate roofs and terracotta ridge pieces. Inserted openings such as those on the north gable of the Electric Press building are in deep metal sub-frames to establish them as contemporary insertions.

The new theatre clad in Portland stone and brick is of a contemporary character and expresses internal social and circulation spaces. Its scale responds to its civic use and acknowledges its civic context.

The events teams for Millennium Square have access to the large BBC screen designed to fit the face of the new theatre. Transmissions from the nearby Town Hall and other spaces as well as BBC material produce a continuity of interest to visitors, users of the Square and passers-by.

The whole project was enabled by positive dialogue with the Royal Fine Art Commission and its successor, CABE, and with English Heritage and Leeds Civic Trust.

Project Sign-off

This diverse but singular group of buildings was required to respond to a very demanding brief. The project contains leisure, commercial, educational and community uses. It has a civic role in the context of Millennium Square whilst responding to the liveliness and media requirements associated with a public events space.

The view from the theatre bar and foyer spaces onto the scene of winter skaters on Millennium Square illustrates the rich range of experiences which the project has brought to the Civic Quarter of Leeds City Centre.

PROJECT TEAM

Client/Building Owner: **Leeds City Council and St James Securties**

Architect: **Panter Hudspith**

Client Architect: **Leeds Civic Architect**

Multi-disciplinary design team for Theatre fit out: **Leeds Design Services Agency / Leeds City Council**

Main Contractor: **Quarmby Construction**

Development of the South Concourse in the 1960s rendered its northern counterpart redundant. Its access to City Square was blocked, and it became a covered car park for executive rail users.

NORTH CONCOURSE, LEEDS CITY RAILWAY STATION

CAREYJONES ARCHITECTS

City Square, Leeds

Construction Value: £2.25 million
Completion Date: August 1998

Description

Refurbishment of the existing 1930s Art Deco railway concourse, together with the construction of new retail units, passenger drop-off and short-stay car park.

History

The North Concourse was built to link two existing railway stations, operated by The London Midland and Scottish (LMS) and the London and North Eastern Railway (LNER). It was open on one side to the platforms and allowed passengers to exit directly onto City Square. The Concourse also linked to the Art Deco Queens Hotel, which itself formed the major focus of City Square as it still does today.

Development of the South Concourse in the 1960s rendered its northern counterpart redundant. Its access to City Square was blocked, and it became a covered car park for executive rail users.

Client's Brief

The brief was to refurbish the listed North Concourse building and re-establish its connection with City Square – as well as adding retail units, visitor drop-off and a short-stay car park. The proposals were to accord with ongoing changes to Leeds' road network, and the station was to remain fully operational during the construction period.

Design Process

The North Concourse forms part of the redevelopment of Leeds City Station, the result of a complex development agreement between Railtrack plc and Teesland Development Company (Northern) Limited.

In the early 1990s, Railtrack was in a position – through the reorganisation of some of their operational land – to effectively release a commercial-development site to a development partner in exchange for refurbishment of the North Concourse.

At this time, Leeds City Council were undertaking major roadworks around Leeds, creating a one-way inner-city 'loop' road in an effort to remove traffic from this area. The access route for private vehicles to the station did not accord with this strategy, and so there was a proposal to relocate the main access for private vehicle/passenger drop-off adjacent to the site proposed for office development – at the same time taking advantage of the necessity to re-route the existing access drive. This relocation of the access went hand-in-hand with the aspiration to redevelop the existing 1930s North Concourse into a contemporary shopping mall, which was considered fundamental to realising the full potential of the Railtrack site.

Extensive negotiations were also held with the local planning authorities, and were initially kick-started by the Leeds Development Corporation with associated grant assistance.

Tremendous interest was generated, from many parties, in the redevelopment of the Concourse building. The Railway Heritage Trust advised that, in their opinion, this was the most important piece of Art Deco railway architecture in the country, and, as such, a substantial grant was obtained for the refurbishment of many of its original features. The Listed Building Officer was similarly interested in the Concourse – especially given the fact that many of the features were original fitments, enabling a very thorough and sensitive refurbishment job to be undertaken.

Extensive research was conducted regarding the 1930s fabric, and where possible many of the original subcontractors were appointed to undertake the refurbishment works, keeping alterations to a

ALL IMAGES ON THIS SPREAD COURTESY OF CAREYJONES ARCHITECTS

minimum. Drawn Metal, the original bronze display-case manufacturers, were appointed to revise the existing cases, allowing the introduction of shop fronts to the west elevation of the Concourse. The arcing rear wall to the new single-storey retail units was built to form a backdrop to the short-stay car park and screen some of the more unsightly existing canopy structures. The original manufacturer of the glass rooflights, Luxcrete, was appointed to provide replacement units; the organisation responsible for the original fibrous-plaster coffered ceiling was traced, in order that these works could be refurbished to the original specification; and the original pendant light fittings were refurbished, with new units built to match where missing.

Other new additions internally saw the introduction of services containment, built to match the fibrous plaster design. The flooring was replaced with ceramic tiles, selecting colours and designs sympathetic to the original proposals, and ramps were included to comply with then-current access regulations.

Building design commenced in January 1993, with LCC approval received that spring. Price negotiations concluded in late 1997, and a start was made on site early in 1998. The work was completed in August 1998.

Project Sign-off

Tenant interest in the retail units created was considerable, given that the reopening of the North Concourse entrance onto City Square was bound to generate considerable footfall in addition to that created by access routes to both long- and short-stay car parks. This interest is reflected in the current tenant list, which includes McDonald's, J D Wetherspoon, WHSmith and the like.

The North Concourse and adjacent Princes Exchange contracts can thus be seen as quite a boost for redevelopment in this quarter of Leeds, and it has successfully promoted the area as a destination in itself rather than as purely a corridor leading to the railway station.

Railtrack's redevelopment of Leeds City Station has included extension to railway platforms, provision of new platform canopies and elevated walkways, additional trackwork to ease previous congestion and associated rail signalling. The total project cost was £245 million, and whilst the works to the North Concourse and associated car parks has only been a fraction of this figure it is this work that has been used to promote the entire station redevelopment, since the trackside and signalling works are far less 'visible' to the everyday user.

Elsewhere, the North Concourse/Princes Exchange developments were a catalyst for further development work currently on site on the upstream banks of the River Aire, where yet more development is in progress.

PROJECT TEAM

Client/Building Owner: **Teesland Development (Northern) Limited**
Architect: **careyjones architects**
Structural Engineer: **WSP (formerly HJT Consulting Engineers)**
Services Engineer: **William E Hannen & Associates**
Main Contractor: **Kier Northern Limited**
Architectural Metalwork: **Drawn Metal**
Rooflight Manufacture: **Luxcrete**

111

ALL IMAGES ON THIS SPREAD BY WWW.JH-JPHOTO.CO.UK

THE ROUND FOUNDRY, HOLBECK URBAN VILLAGE
BUILDING DESIGN PARTNERSHIP

Water Lane, Holbeck, Leeds

Construction Value: Phase 1: £10 million
                           Phase 2: £4 million
Completion Date: Phase 1: March 2004
                           Phase 2: May 2008

Description

The idea of creating an urban village in the former
industrial area of Holbeck was proposed and
championed by the Leeds Architects and Design
Initiative (LADI). A planning framework to create the
village was adopted by the City Council in 1999.
The Round Foundry was the first significant development
to take place.

The repair and adaptive re-use of a group of redundant
historic structures and the construction of new infill
buildings to create a mixed-use development. Part of
the goal of this particular refurbishment is to ensure
the regeneration of a whole area, including better
opportunities for the nearby residents.

History

Holbeck, located to the south of the city centre, was
originally an industrial suburb of Leeds. The Round
Foundry was established in 1796 as the country's
second specialist engineering works, and remained in
this use throughout the 19th century. In the late 20th
century, industrial uses declined and the area became
run-down, dilapidated and underused.

Client's Brief

The client required a phased mixed-use development
that would express both the historic character of
the area and its regeneration through a mixture of
carefully conserved historic fabric and attractive
contemporary elements. The quality of the design was
seen as essential in creating a market where none had
previously existed.

Design Process

As Britain's only surviving first-generation engineering
works, the Round Foundry was well known in Leeds
as a pioneering site of national historical significance.

However, the area had the unfortunate appearance of
a jumble of dilapidated old buildings. Leeds architects
Regan Miller prepared concept proposals to generate
interest in the site, and developer CTP St James decided
to become involved and embarked on a process of
site assembly. Regan Miller were not able to take the
project forward, and the Manchester office of BDP was
appointed. A masterplan and Stage C (outline design)
proposals for the whole development have been followed
by phased implementation.

The site contains seven listed buildings together with
major archaeological remains, all located within the
Holbeck Conservation Area. The design process followed
the practice of 'informed conservation'. A detailed and
ongoing assessment of standing and buried industrial
archaeology, which was a planning requirement,
established a clear understanding of the significance of
the site as a whole and in its constituent parts. During
this exercise, it was possible to confirm those parts of
the complex that must be retained and those parts that
it would be preferable to demolish.

With the exception of a large mid-19th-century
engineering workshop, the retained buildings are two or
three storeys in height and small to medium in scale.
They are of an industrial-vernacular character, generally
constructed from a mixture of handmade and machine-
made brick walls under pitched slated roofs. The original
layout of the buildings around external yards linked by
pedestrian passageways was a major influence in the
project design.

The conservation philosophy was to repair existing fabric
on a like-for-like basis using matching materials and
techniques. Contemporary interventions and extensions
to existing buildings are in a modern idiom, contextual in
scale but clearly differentiated from the historic buildings

in material and detail. This approach of layering the modern adaptive works onto the conserved historic fabric exploits the qualities of each era, to produce a new place which has evolved from the old.

The resulting form of the development is therefore of small- to medium-scaled buildings grouped around a series of defined spaces of varying size which are linked by pedestrian routes. Variety is given by the juxtaposition of modern and historical forms and materials. High-quality paving materials, external lighting, signage and text explaining the historical significance of the Round Foundry create an attractive public realm.

The northwestern portion of the site comprises a series of apartment buildings, mostly new but including one converted structure. This part of the development was sold to a residential developer, Crosby Homes, who went on to complete its detailed design and construction. Elsewhere there is a mixture of office, residential, retail and restaurant uses.

The first-phase construction works were carried out between January 2002 and March 2004. A small intermediate phase followed in 2005 and a third phase was completed in May 2008. This will leave the construction of two new buildings in the southeastern corner of the site to complete the project. The development has been sold to Igloo Regeneration Partnership.

Project Sign-off

The Round Foundry has demonstrated what can be achieved through informed conservation, high-quality design, a creative and determined developer and a constructive planning authority. In the context of the wider Holbeck Urban Village Initiative, a vibrant nucleus has been created. This has attracted architects, designers, professional and legal businesses, government agencies, new-media businesses, residents, restaurants, bars and shops. A market has been created where none previously existed, and this has given great confidence to developers of surrounding sites.

The most significant effects of the Initiative are that what, at first sight, appear to be nondescript buildings and places can become commercially successful and culturally attractive places; and that this comes about through a process of evolution – the new emerging from the old – rather than a process of complete change through site clearance, in which context and continuity are lost.

The principles which informed the Round Foundry development can be applied to many other sites. In this way, the Round Foundry can become a reference point and exemplar from which other parts of Leeds can benefit.

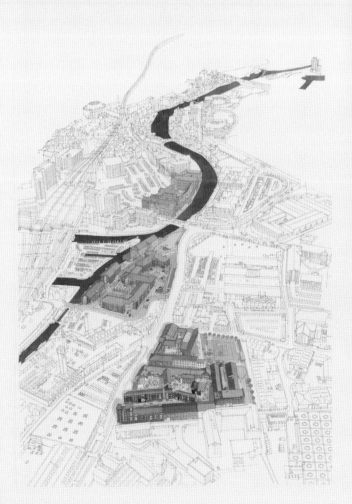

PROJECT TEAM

Client/Building Owner: **CTP St James /
Igloo Regeneration Partnership**

Architect: **Building Design Partnership**

Quantity Surveyor: **Rex Proctor & Partners**

Structural Engineer: **SJEC Consulting Engineers Ltd**

Services Engineer: **Phase 1 John Ryan Partnership and Ernest
Griffiths Consulting Engineers**

Main Contractor:
Phase 1: Quarmby Construction Limited

Phase 2a: Simpsons of York

Phase 2b: William Birch & Company

By creating the new arcade level, the design has allowed the retail units on the external Headrow façade to extend beneath the internal street, thus creating the deeper retail floorplates required by modern users.

THE LIGHT

DLG ARCHITECTS

The Headrow, Leeds

Construction Value: £55 million
Completion Date: Spring 2002

Description

The development of a mixed-use leisure and retail centre in the heart of Leeds city centre, combining new-build with the renovation of two listed buildings.

History

The two existing listed structures, Permanent House and the Headrow Buildings, formed part of the original Headrow project; their designs featured in the competition-winning proposals by Sir Reginald Blomfield and they were built between 1929 and 1931 in conjunction with Leeds architects, G. W. Atkinson. More recently the site had been developed by Leeds Permanent Building Society, and included the 18-storey Albion Tower (known locally as 'K2') and the offices of Leeds City Council Planning Department.

Client's Brief

The brief, developed in conjunction with the architectural team, was to provide an integrated, multi-level, mixed-use scheme that responded to the urban-regeneration needs of the site, improved permeability and provided a fusion of uses that would ensure future commercial sustainability.

Design Process

There were several important factors that had to be addressed to enable the successful design to be developed. To allow improved public permeability throughout the site, part of the original street pattern needed to be reopened. There were also a number of significant level changes, both on the surrounding streets and within the listed buildings themselves, which had to be resolved. In addressing these constraints, a plan developed which took advantage of the level changes by effectively having two ground-floor spaces: the arcade, which is accessed from Albion Street; and the lower courtyard, which is reached through the original Headrow arch as well as from St Anne's Street and the Cathedral

and from Cookridge Street.

To enable the Albion Street entrance and arcade to be introduced, a major reworking of the rear Headrow façade was undertaken in order to raise the original street by one level. Whilst significant reconstruction of the rear façade was undertaken, its striking historical glazing pattern – one of the earliest examples of curtain-walling construction – has been maintained. This helps to re-emphasise the early steel-frame nature of the building. By creating the new arcade level, the design has allowed the retail units on the external Headrow façade to extend beneath the internal street, thus creating the deeper retail floorplates required by modern users.

In establishing the main circulation within the arcade and courtyard, the development has introduced and reinforced some striking city-centre views, of both the Headrow Buildings' arch and the neighbouring St Anne's Cathedral. A simple six-storey-high glazed screen encloses the courtyard and opens up dramatic views of the Cathedral. The materials used within the public spaces are selected to complement the listed buildings' fabric and to emphasise the 'street' nature of the space. The use of natural limestone flooring, external-type street lighting for night-time and natural light for the spaces in daytime all combine to this effect. They also help to integrate these new arcades into Leeds' street pattern and provide a high-quality environment into which the

118

many internal restaurants and leisure uses can spill out, blurring the division of internal and external space within the scheme.

An important element for the success of the design has been the integration of the multi-level spaces internally. Vital to the success of these spaces was the introduction of clear vertical circulation routes to provide strong visibility throughout the scheme. This has been successfully developed – for example, the circulation for the 13-screen cinema complex has been introduced within the arcade itself, providing interest and movement throughout the day. The introduction of lightweight glazed bridges further emphasises movement throughout the spaces and provides a contemporary link between the new construction and the original listed fabric.

The glazed roof covering the arcade and courtyard provides a simple and elegant curved enclosure, allowing natural light to flood into the spaces below and provide an ever-changing environment of sunlight and shadows.

Project Sign-off

In fulfilling both the commercial and regeneration aspects of its wider brief, The Light has been successful in a number of areas. Before the project commenced, the site itself had become something of a barrier to successful regeneration in the area. Within it, elements of the old street pattern had been blocked off, effectively preventing public access through a whole city block.

The introduction of the new arcades has reconnected the street pattern and, indeed, now acts as an important public route providing good connections through to the developments in Millennium Square. The creation of new public covered space reflects the arcade tradition of Victorian Leeds and also allows the public to access and interact with the important historic buildings of the Headrow, Permanent House and St Anne's Cathedral.

DLG ARCHITECTS

PROJECT TEAM

Client/Building Owner: **HBOS, in joint venture with Clerical Medical Investment Group**

Development Manager: **St James Securities Ltd**

Architect: **DLG Architects**

Quantity Surveyor: **Cyril Sweets**

Structural Engineer: **White Young Green**

M+E Engineers: **John Ryan Partnership**

Main Contractor: **Bovis Lend Lease Limited – Northern Division**

119

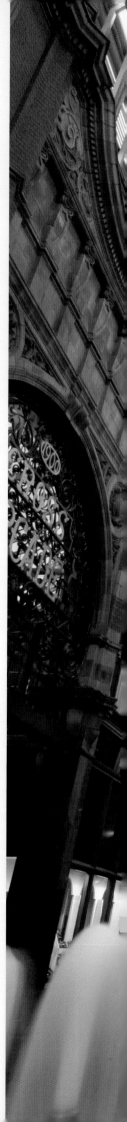

VICTORIA QUARTER, LEEDS

LATHAMS

County Arcade, Cross Arcade and Queen Victoria Street

Construction Value: £7 million
Completion Date: 1990

Description

The sensitive but spirited restoration of one of Leeds' most opulent Edwardian shopping arcades, incorporating an adjoining shopping street to form an entirely new civic 'Quarter'.

History

County and Cross Arcades were the most sumptuous of Leeds' Edwardian shopping arcades, built around the Empire Theatre with which they share some of their florid decor. Completed in 1904, they were designed, along with the theatre and surrounding streets, by Britain's most prolific theatre architect of the period, Frank Matcham.

By the mid-1980s, however, the arcades were creaking with age and had received a drastic overlay of plastic-and-neon shop fascias. They were also losing trade to the newer, 'artificial' shopping malls in the West End of the city.

Client's Brief

The owners of the arcades, Prudential, decided it was time for a comprehensive revamp and invited proposals from architects and interior designers. The conservation-based architects Lathams ensured a thoroughly accurate job in restoring Matcham's masterpiece, but their clinching concept was to continue in Leeds' grand retail tradition and create a brand new 'prime' shopping arcade by including the adjacent Queen Victoria Street and roofing it over with glass.

Design Process

The proposal was achieved by covering over Queen Victoria Street with a new glazed roof in a modern but 'empathetic' manner, in order to double the covered retail area; and by the development of appropriate fire strategies. Within the arcades themselves work involved the repair and cleaning of original terracotta faience finishes; the painting of ironwork to a new colour scheme; the careful restoration of all Edwardian mahogany shopfronts; and high-quality design and workmanship in the paving, landscaping and fittings to Queen Victoria Street. Signage and graphics were rigorously controlled, and artists were employed – a sculptor/blacksmith for new light fittings, seats and kiosks; a sculpture mason for the fountain; a ceramic artist for the terrazzo flooring; and a stained-glass artist for the roof. A lettings policy was adopted which created a balanced mix of tenants, and the area as a whole was promoted with a new identity: 'The Victoria Quarter'.

Planning permission from a sceptical Leeds City Council was not easy, but finally gained after support was given by the Royal Fine Art Commission.

Working from Matcham's tantalisingly sketchy original drawings and a handful of early photographs, the architects set about scheduling all repairs to each shopfront based on a series of photocopied drawings.

The first task was to clean all exposed walls. Repairs were then carried out that entailed lifting all faience copings and re-fixing them, using a total of no fewer than 2,600 stainless-steel pins. Small screw-holes and cracks were patched with colour-matching epoxy resin.

Nearly all the mahogany-and-glass shopfronts needed total renewal. Fortunately, an original example – the superb Chapman's Corsetieres – remained in pristine condition, and served as a model for hand-carving the ornate mahogany frames and reproducing the original gilded Art Nouveau lettering.

Restoration was not without some judicious fakery. To the architects' relief, even Matcham's revered original revealed its share of cost-cutting artifice. For instance,

what were assumed to be ornate mahogany finials within each shopfront were in fact cast-and-painted plaster.

The overriding problem was means of escape from fire. The local fire authority insisted that each shop inside the arcade had two separate means of escape. An elaborate system incorporating two levels of fire compartments, automatic smoke vents and a maze of fire escapes was devised. The galleries have now been connected up into a continuous passageway by forming two new bridges across the arcades.

In Lathams' pattern of things, repairs plus the occasional extrapolation (such as the new gallery bridge) were carried out to the letter of Matcham's original, whereas new insertions were freely and creatively designed in the spirit of Matcham's embellishments – as was the case with the new stained glass, mosaics and wrought ironwork.

At the Victoria Quarter, 'sympathetic but contemporary' means that the new artistic insertions have a presence of their own within the flamboyant ethos established by Matcham. The crafted new elements culminate in Brian Clarke's breathtaking technicoloured stained-glass roof to the new arcade in Queen Victoria Street. Totalling 750 m^2 in area, it was the largest secular commission of stained-glass windows in the world and was described in Clarke's own words as 'an unending floor of liquid colour'.

The other art elements are less flamboyant: mosaic roundels set in the floor of the restored County Arcade were designed by Joanna Veevers; and the wrought-iron lamp pendants, litter bins and gates by blacksmiths Alan Dawson and Jim Horrobin.

The result contains both a regular pattern that fits into a repetitive building fabric and a richness of design

and colour that matches, but does not mimic, Matcham's decor.

Project Sign-off

The County Arcade and neighbouring streets form a direct link between the office area to the west and the extensive markets and bus station to the east. With a constant throughput of potential customers, it would be hard to imagine a better location for shops. The intent was to make the arcades and streets a destination as well as a route.

Hence the new arcade, which encourages passers-by to linger by protecting them from the elements. Even more inviting are the café restaurants that spill out onto the pavement within the new arcade.

The refurbished Victoria Quarter now contains a double core of glorious arcades, and it has a much more amorphous edge which merges into the surrounding city fabric. The Victoria Quarter's success (including Harvey Nichols) is now expanding by an organic 'ripple effect' to rejuvenate surrounding areas of the city centre.

PROJECT TEAM

Client/Building Owner: **Prudential plc**
Architect: **Lathams**
Quantity Surveyor: **Roger Rowlinson Associates**
Structural Engineer: **Deakin Callard & Partners**
Services Engineer: **Brian Ford Partnership**
Main Contractor: **Mowlem Plc**

The design process entailed a substantial amount of historical research, and negotiation with the multiple owners of the spaces in order to allow the city council to adopt them.

THE BRIGGATE YARDS AND ALLEYS REFURBISHMENT
PLANNING DEPARTMENT, LEEDS CITY COUNCIL

A series of yards and alleys off Briggate, central Leeds

Construction Value: Unknown
Completion Date: 1994

Description

The refurbishment of these yards and alleys involved re-paving, the removal of vehicle-parking spaces and other clutter, improved street lighting and the introduction of public art.

History

The yards and alleys developed out of medieval burgage plots at the rear of properties fronting onto Briggate, which by the 18th century had been fully infilled around relatively narrow access routes off Briggate itself. By the late 20th century, these had largely ceased to function as pedestrian routes and had become little more than dumping grounds for rubbish.

Client's Brief

The brief was to refurbish the yards and alleys so that they once again became safe and attractive spaces for pedestrians to use, whilst retaining and reinforcing their historic character.

Design Process

The proposals for the yards and alleys were made by the former Planning Department of Leeds City Council (now part of the Development Department). The Planning Department also undertook the negotiations with the private owners and provided the funding. The work was undertaken by the council's former Highways Department (now part of the Development Department).

The design process entailed a substantial amount of historical research, and negotiation with the multiple owners of the spaces in order to allow the city council to adopt them. As part of this process owners were persuaded, where appropriate, to remove or resite air-conditioning plants, to store their refuse internally and to re-orientate their ground-floor commercial activities to include frontages onto the yards and alleys – for example,

the City Varieties Theatre on Swan Street.

The resulting proposals included the removal of car parking on Swan Street; re-paving throughout using new stone setts and flags, tumbled and flamed to provide an aged appearance; refurbishing the surviving gas lamps; and updating the electric street lighting with a soft form of light that was similar in character to the original gas lighting. Public art, including that in Swan Street, was also incorporated into the scheme.

Over half a million pounds of public-sector funding was made available for the project, which in turn levered out a significant amount of private-sector investment in the upgrading of the adjacent buildings. The work was undertaken over a period in the early 1990s.

Project Sign-off

The yards and alleys are now well used by pedestrians as a result of their looking attractive, feeling safe and offering a different experience to the wide and busy streets such as Briggate itself.

However, this programme of work also helped contribute to a remarkable change in the fortunes of Briggate as a shopping street. It went, within a period of a few years in the mid-1990s, from being a location chiefly for charity and discount stores to welcoming the first Harvey Nichols store outside London, together with a number of other exclusive fashion outlets.

WWW.JH-JPHOTO.CO.UK

WWW.JH-JPHOTO.CO.UK

PROJECT TEAM

Client/Building Owner: **Leeds City Council**
Architect: **Planning Department, Leeds City Council**
Main Contractor: **Highways Department, Leeds City Council**

HIDDEN LEEDS

Every city has its hidden side, those parts off the beaten track where only the lost or the knowing stray. Hidden Leeds is unexpected Leeds. Consider the town halls: apart from Brodrick's magnificent Leeds Town Hall on Victoria Square there are more modest examples in the city's hinterland, notably at Wetherby, Yeadon and Morley.

Each of these three is a proud demonstration of 19th-century civic pride, ranging from the modest Classicism of the Wetherby building of 1845 to the almost bombastic example of 1895 at Morley, which – with its portico, pediment, pilasters and surmounting tower – makes an obvious gesture towards its precursor at Leeds. No longer debating chambers for elected representation, they remain as reminders of the civic worth of these satellite communities.

Hidden Leeds is unseen Leeds. At the top of Woodhouse Lane where buses used to run down University Road, students now fill the street. Here can be found Alfred Waterhouse buildings for the Yorkshire College of Science, begun in 1877. Red-brick and terracotta-tiled, the Great Hall and the later Clothworkers' Court are just the sort of edifices which

www.leedsinnovationcentre.co.uk

^ Leeds University – the original Yorkshire College buildings
WWW.JH-JPHOTO.CO.UK

^ Leeds University Great Hall
and Clothworkers Court
WWW.JH-JPHOTO.CO.UK

>> Leeds University Woodhouse
Cemetery, Greek Revival Chapel
WWW.JH-JPHOTO.CO.UK

gave the red-brick universities their nickname. But a close examination of the inscriptions and iconography will show these buildings to be fine expressions of northern pride. A little further down the hill are the modern administrative and science buildings designed by Chamberlin, Powell and Bon in 1965. To many these are the epitome of the 'concrete jungle', but to the discerning eye they are in fact the prototype of the marvellous Barbican complex in the City of London.

Hidden Leeds is forgotten Leeds. Behind tall walls and big buildings, the most unlikely things can still be found. The Woodhouse Cemetery of 1835 has now been absorbed within the university campus, but here, where the headstones have been bulldozed into mass graves or laid out as pathways to be forever trampled beneath passing feet, a quiet patch of green remains. John Clark designed the gate lodge and chapel in the Greek Revival style, for what was originally the Leeds General Cemetery: the one Tuscan in antis and the other tetrastyle Ionic. Symbols of death remain in the urns which surmount the gatehouse, and in its blank windows which stare fixedly like dead eyes. Similar connotations of death were found in the Egyptian temple style, so it is all the more surprising that three years later the paternalistic John Marshall – who, with Thomas Babington Macaulay, was one of the two original MPs for Leeds following the Reform Act of 1832 – allowed Ignatius Bonomi to employ the Egyptian style for his new Temple Mills on Marshall Street. Complete with hefty lotus columns, battered walls and obelisk-chimneys, this is about the most unlikely former flax-spinning mill to be found anywhere. Somehow it has survived, and its location within the new Holbeck Urban Village must ensure its future.

^ Leeds University
WWW.JH-JPHOTO.CO.UK

> Marshall's Temple
Mills, Holbeck
WWW.JH-JPHOTO.CO.UK

>> Holbeck
Urban Village
WWW.JH-JPHOTO.CO.UK

The integrity of the original Arts-and-Crafts-style house had to be maintained whilst retaining the freedom to create a dramatic contemporary addition, linked to the house but primarily related to the rear garden space.

30 NORTH PARADE

BAUMAN LYONS ARCHITECTS LIMITED IN ASSOCIATION WITH MAGGIE PICKLES

30 North Parade, West Park, Leeds

Construction Value: £57 thousand
Completion Date: January 2004

Description

The construction of a single-storey garden room, with garage behind, adjacent to an existing large semi-detached Edwardian house.

History

The client lives in a five-bedroom Edwardian home in West Park, one of the northern suburbs of Leeds.

Client's Brief

The client felt that the house lacked a sense of connection to its rear garden, the sunniest area of which was occupied by an old garage. The brief was to relocate the garage to the north-facing driveway, alongside the house, and create a new garden room, which formed an enclosure but was essentially an extension of the garden.

Design Process

The decision was taken early on in the design evolution to build a separate garden room rather than create an extension. The integrity of the original Arts-and-Crafts-style house had to be maintained whilst retaining the freedom to create a dramatic contemporary addition, linked to the house but primarily related to the rear garden space. The garage at the front, by contrast, was to present a traditional aspect in keeping with the Edwardian street scene. Care was taken in the detailing and use of materials on the two 'faces' of the building to ensure that the transition from traditional to contemporary was sensitive and appropriate. Indeed, whilst the decorative 'trimmings' of the Arts and Crafts house have not been copied in the garden room, the honest expression of form and materials in the latter is very much in the spirit of the movement.

Essentially, the garden room is formed by an aluminium-clad monopitched cantilevered roof resting on blockwork

walls to the side and rear. Frameless glazed walls complete the other two sides of the space, which, along with a partly mirrored fourth wall, make the 4 by 3 m room appear larger and dissolve notions of internal and external space. This illusion is strengthened by continuing the room's stone flooring seamlessly onto a sweeping terrace, which is partly sheltered by the overhanging roof, and by extending the minimal white internal wall with its stainless-steel skirting detail along the length of the outside rendered boundary wall. In order to achieve the roof cantilever, a structural channel section had to be tied back to the existing house. This channel is also used to support a lightweight glass canopy, which shelters the connection from the existing door in the bay window to the new room. This carefully considered connection ties the two buildings together compositionally, and creates a dialogue between the existing bay window and the new room. The terrace was also extended across the back of the house to ground the whole composition to the garden. Locally sourced textured millstone grit was finally selected in order to visually link the new elements to the original house.

The client comments:

'From the start, the collaborative relationship involving the builder, the architects, and ourselves has been one of the pleasures of the scheme and an unexpected bonus. This enabled the building to 'evolve' on-site to the satisfaction of all parties.'

The project commenced in August 2003 and took five months on site.

ALL IMAGES ON THIS SPREAD MARTINE HAMILTON KNIGHT/BUILT VISION

Project Sign-off

This project is the result of what proved to be an engaging and highly pleasurable collaborative process between architect, client and contractor. The quality of the built environment depends as much on the care and sensitivity with which people adapt their own homes as on larger civic gestures. Hidden 'jewels' such as this highlight the importance of good design in an environment in which many people live, but which is often overlooked when talking of a city's development.

The project won a commendation in the RIBA White Rose Awards in 2005.

PROJECT TEAM

Client/Building Owner: **Tony and Anne Ray**
Architect: **Bauman Lyons Architects Limited (with Maggie Pickles)**
Quantity Surveyor: **Bernard Williams Associates**
Structural Engineer: **Capita Symmonds**
Main Contractor: **Fielding and Jackson**

The building is organised around
a central covered street, providing
a strong focal point for social
interaction, circulation, display and
ad hoc meeting.

CARDINAL HEENAN CATHOLIC HIGH SCHOOL

AEDAS ARCHITECTS LIMITED

Tongue Lane, Leeds

Construction Value: £9 million
Completion Date: 2000

Description

This new 900-pupil secondary school in the Meanwood district of north Leeds replaces existing school buildings within the site curtilage. Construction overlapped with continued use of the existing school, enabling a smooth transfer on completion.

History

Outline planning permission for the project was inherited, and stipulated means of access which, in turn, determined the building plot. Also included was an illustrative building and site layout, which simply put all cars to the road side of the building, leaving a gap to the east for external play and a social area.

Client's Brief

The arrangement detailed above was felt by the client to be too simplistic given the opportunity afforded by the site, which sits almost at the crown of a hill with wide views southwards to the city. Accordingly, the diagram was reversed, locating cars and services to the north and external play and social area to the south. This enabled both building and external areas to take maximum advantage of sun and view.

Design Process

The building is organised around a central covered street, providing a strong focal point for social interaction, circulation, display and ad hoc meeting. More than a school corridor, this street is glazed, light and responsive to surrounding activities, expressing its central social role. It is unheated, but the naturally ventilated glass roof ensures it will be usable year-round, forming a buffer zone.

The 'defining move' of the design is to bend this street into a horseshoe shape, enabling two entrances – for independent school and community use – to be

approached from the same point and lead into the street at either end. It suggests a basic strategy of school-only (daytime) and school/community (evening) functions.

A social nucleus was incorporated, accommodating entrance, reception, hall, dining and other social spaces at the heart of the building. This nucleus is extended across the street to the library, itself an academic focus for the school.

Street and core are united by a structure of radiating glued laminated beams incorporating bolted flitch plates to improve span:depth ratios, combined with 75 mm thick planked roofing to achieve spans of up to 4.8 m. The resultant irregular plan-form is roofed flat using a non-PVC-based single-ply membrane on tapered insulation.

Inset from one end, at the focal point of the northern landscape design and signalled by a zinc-clad staircase, the street widens to an entrance foyer. The leading end of the street is then available for the chapel, its curved locally sourced dry-stone wall signifying this important space whilst encouraging the visitor around to the main entrance.

At this point, the religious and secular content of the school interact. This relationship, of chapel as religious focus terminating the street as social focus, mirrors a traditional social status, and helps bond the physical structure of the building to the ethos of the school.

Another driving force of Cardinal Heenan School is the status of independent departments. The words 'ownership' and 'territory' quoted from the design brief help explain this status. Hence each department on plan is fairly clearly defined, extending as 'fingers' from the street, and each affording outward extension.

ALL IMAGES ON THIS SPREAD ARE COURTESY OF AEDAS ARCHITECTS LTD.

These fingers enclose sheltered courtyards for social and recreational use which are protected from traffic, south facing and have extensive views. Most classrooms take advantage of this orientation via bay windows, the internal space protected from glare and heat-gain by external louvred solar shading. Standing-seam pitched aluminium roofing at various orientations engages with the flat-roofed core — overhangs enhance the plan dynamics whilst sheltering walls below. A consistent use of materials, colours and textures unifies the whole, based upon 'honest' material representation, but technically there is no 'big idea' which dominates and the building is not subsumed in statements about building technique.

One of the architects' key concerns was natural light, and its varied use to illuminate as well as differentiate spaces and raise the spirit of the institution. So, for example, the building has larger window assemblies at its entrances and at viewpoints from public areas to the outside; rooflighting to the street; clerestories to classroom corridors, with borrowed supplementary light to classrooms; and neutral northlights to the sports hall. Windows are composite aluminium/timber for thermal, lifecycle and visual reasons.

Project Sign-off

The new Cardinal Heenan Catholic High School was the first Voluntary Aided School to be procured under the Private Finance Initiative (PFI) and has been identified by the Commission for Architecture and the Built Environment (CABE) as a 'benchmark' project.

Its design attempts to give built form to the school's ethos, specifically the status of the individual and group within the school and their relationship to the wider

community. Principles developed through the project included examining the idea of the school as 'settlement in microcosm'; exploring hierarchies which help define individual, class, departmental or whole-school spaces, leading to a clearer sense of social structure; developing each part of the building to suit its particular function; and locating the project firmly in its context.

PROJECT TEAM

Client/Building Owner: **Cardinal Heenan Catholic High School**
Architect: **Aedas Architects Limited**
Quantity Surveyor: **Gleeds**
Structural Engineer: **Buro Happold**
Services Engineer: **Buro Happold**
Main Contractor: **Jarvis Construction (UK) Limited**

Initial ideas evolved around the use of the 'Segal style' timber-frame construction method suited to the skills of the group, the steeply sloping site and the desire to use materials with minimal environmental impact.

THREE ECO HOUSES

LEEDS ENVIRONMENTAL DESIGN ASSOCIATES LIMITED (LEDA)

11A–C Allerton Park, Leeds

Construction Value: £120 thousand
Completion Date: 1997

Description

A terrace of three new self-build timber-framed houses. Two are five-bedroomed; the remaining dwelling has three bedrooms.

History

The site was the abandoned garden of the adjacent house (No. 13 Allerton Park). Allerton Park is a tree-lined circular drive of large properties dating from the late 19th century to the present. The new buildings respond to the scale of the adjacent dwellings by appearing as one large house.

Client's Brief

The group of self-builders employed sustainable materials, including timber frame, and sought to use their skills – including joinery and architecture – to address the issues of: water conservation, including greywater recycling and composting toilets; high thermal performance of building fabric; and low CO_2 outputs in use and construction. The aim was to achieve a healthy indoor environment and to create replacement habitat with the introduction of green roofs.

Design Process

This was a collaborative project, with each household helping to determine the means of construction and overall design. Architectural design was provided by Jonathan Lindh, working closely with the group members – with particular design input from Heimir Salt.

Initial ideas evolved around the use of the 'Segal style' timber-frame construction method suited to the skills of the group, the steeply sloping site and the desire to use materials with minimal environmental impact. It required, for example, far less concrete for foundations than a conventional masonry structure. The theme of water conservation also became a major design generator. An 'autonomous' approach was adopted for water services

and sewerage, using rainwater collection, greywater recycling and composting toilets.

Use of local materials was a high priority, in order to minimise the environmental impact arising from transportation. One of the group members owned a wood containing larch trees that were used for the cladding.

The design responds to the natural surroundings of Gledhow Valley, which cuts a green swathe through the suburban area of Chapel Allerton. The planted roof was incorporated to increase habitat and replace the area of garden occupied by the new building footprint. Wood was always intended to be the predominant cladding material as well as forming the main construction. The aim was to strike a balance between fitting in with the area and clearly stating the ethos of the design visually.

The planners were enthusiastic about the environmental agenda set for the project, and extensive pre-application consultation took place. However, the use of a planted roof – and timber to the front elevations facing Allerton Park as well as to the sides – was not acceptable to the planners as a response to the streetscape. The amended design thus gave a more conventional face to the street and referenced the Edwardian vernacular of the adjacent houses, though one of these has now been demolished and replaced by a refreshingly modern block of apartments.

The construction method allowed the group to share the building of the main frames and roof. Thereafter each household concentrated on their own dwelling, with some sharing of resources. The construction of the reed bed and pond for the water-treatment system and the greywater recycling filter system was also shared.

Each house has slight variations in construction detailing – types of insulation, roof membranes, timber-window

WWW.JH-JPHOTO.CO.UK

pattern and manufacture – all reflecting personal preference and individual access to particular skills and resources.

The principal materials comprise the main timber frame, boron treated for low environmental impact, and UK-grown timber studs for partitions and infill of external walls. Insulation is formed from recycled newspaper, polystyrene and glass fibre; with thicknesses of 150–200 mm for the walls, 200 mm for the floor and 450 mm for the roof to ensure high thermal performance.

The external cladding is Yorkshire-grown larch-batten, boarding and trims, with white-painted cement-and-cellulose-fibre panels.

WWW.JH-JPHOTO.CO.UK

Timber double- and triple-glazed windows achieve U-values of 1.8 W/m$_2$K, while the insulated timber doors achieve 0.8 W/m$_2$K.

Recycled railway sleepers are used to form retaining walls for the parking and front garden areas. Recycled hardcore with gravel in recycled plastic formers were used to construct the parking area removing the need for conventional drainage.

Project Sign-off

The project commenced on site in 1994, and was completed in 1997.

Internal finishes were mainly timber, with natural paints and stains, and linoleum for the floors.

PROJECT TEAM

Client/Building Owner: **Gledhow Bank Ecohousing Group**
Architect: **J. Lindh (LEDA), H. Salt**
Structural Engineer: **Steve Jones (Melia Smith and Jones)**
Energy Consultant: **Matthew Hill (LEDA)**
Staircase design and joinery: **Nick Arrow**

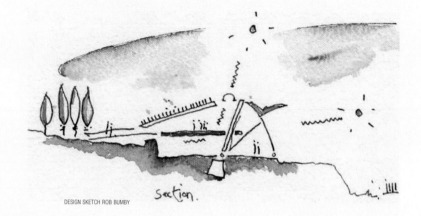

A simple Modernist plan, set against an organic section, was crystallised by an early watercolour sketch showing how the building, set deep into the hillside, would open up its southwestern face towards the sun.

DESIGN SKETCH ROB BUMBY

THE EPICENTRE

OSA ARCHITECTS LEEDS
(FORMERLY ONE STOP ARCHITECTS)

Meanwood Valley Urban Farm, Sugarwell Road, Leeds

Construction Value: £375 thousand
Completion Date: September 1999

Description

The EpiCentre is a two-storey visitors' centre for the Meanwood Valley Urban Farm – with a reception area, exhibition halls, classrooms, office and a wintergarden.

History

Founded in 1980, the urban farm in Meanwood is a very successful enterprise, with an organic market garden, and barns and fields for livestock. The farm is located along the Meanwood Valley Trail, the green route from central Leeds through Meanwood Woods and out to Golden Acre Park.

Client's Brief

The client set out to create a 'green' resource for Leeds, promoting awareness of environmental issues through the sustainable design and construction of the visitors' centre building itself and the exhibitions within it. The building, at the heart of the farm, was to be part of the farm trail, with an information centre for schools and the wider community.

Design Process

Design strategies centred on natural and organic sources of inspiration – an upturned tree with its roots in the air became the visible timber frame. Architecturally, the Walter Segal system, as demonstrated by a completed doctors' surgery near Wetherby, provided the principle of a building 'resting lightly on the earth', easily built by non-specialists and using timber as a sustainable construction material – all appropriate in the context of a farm. A simple Modernist plan, set against an organic section, was crystallised by an early watercolour sketch showing how the building, set deep into the hillside, would open up its southwestern face towards the sun.

The building, at the time designed as the 'greenest' in the UK, owed more to current design responses to urgent

environmental issues than to its local context. Local sourcing of materials, however, was a key principle in the specification process in order to minimise the use of scarce resources and the creation of CO_2 by restricting energy use within manufacture and transport. The larch for the structural timber and the boarding came from the nearby Harewood Estate.

Leeds City Council responded to the match funding required by the Lottery Millennium Fund by contributing the Council's Community Building Firm, an innovative construction-training vehicle for the young unemployed. The post-and-beam structure of nine identical frames were fabricated on site and set on concrete-pad foundations. The frames were infilled on three sides with external walls of timber studding with 200 mm thick Warmcell recycled-newspaper insulation, and clad externally with timber boarding on a breather membrane.

The fully glazed southwest elevation maximises light and heat from the sun. Its outer wall and a second, double-glazed, inner wall set 2 m back – both in recycled aluminium framing – form the wintergarden, designed to pre-heat cold air in winter and to disperse warm air in summer via a row of high-level opening windows. Full-height sliding doors onto the wintergarden allow cross-ventilation with cool air from the north. All other windows are 'eco-plus' timber units with insulating glass. The turf roof, with 300 mm thick Warmcell insulation, oversails the glazed wall, providing shading in summer. The insulated concrete ground-floor slab, partly finished with stone flags, provides a heat store for solar gain.

The design set out to achieve a building with very low environmental costs, by minimising both energy use throughout the year and waste production during construction and the life of the building. A domestic-sized condensing boiler with hot-water radiators tops

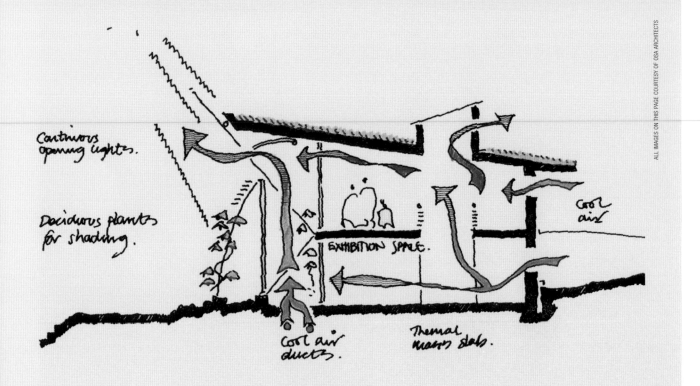

Continuous
opening lights.

Deciduous plants
for shading.

EXHIBITION SPACE.

Cool
air

Cool air
ducts.

Thermal
mass slab.

SUMMER VENTILATION

up the solar gain in winter. The Clivus composting toilet
system – a large tank set under long-drop toilets –
creates usable compost from the aerobic breakdown
of solid waste and stored liquid run-off. Greywater is
processed through reed beds before joining the nearby
beck. Rainwater collected from the roof becomes
drinking water for livestock.

The building stands at the beginning of the farm trail:
the route winds through the reception and ground-floor
display area; through the first-floor exhibition, accessible
via the stair or the glazed platform lift; and out via the
rear exit to the viewing platform, connected by a bridge
to the hillside path.

Following the initial feasibility study the design was
developed over 12 months, with a two and a half year
construction period.

Project Sign-off

The EpiCentre has become a focus for thinking about
sustainability in Leeds, particularly within the city
council – contributing to the ongoing debate amongst
businesses, professionals, students and the wider
community. The development of the Green Strategy for
Leeds in the mid-1990s became the catalyst for the
realisation of the project, enthusiastically promoted
by the director and staff at the farm. The building has
developed a high profile following its official opening
by the then Environment Minister, Michael Meacher,
in 1999, and the visit by Prince Charles in 2002
raised awareness further afield. The work of the farm,
and the building itself, continue to feature in national
publications. The farm is a highly successful resource for
local schools, and continues to develop environmental,
farm and countryside education. The public can tap into
'sustainability' during an enjoyable day out at the farm,
or on a trip along the Meanwood Valley Trail.

PROJECT TEAM

Client/Building Owner: **Sue Reddington,
Director, Meanwood Valley Farm**

Architect: **OSA Architects Leeds (formerly One Stop Architects)**

Design Team: **Rob Bumby and Pamela Parkinson**

Quantity Surveyor: **Leeds Community Building Firm**

Structural Engineer: **GMG Limited, Leeds**

Main Contractor: **Leeds Community Building Firm,
Leeds City Council**

Environmental Consultant: **Leeds Environmental
Design Associates**

143

The building has an intriguing history, stemming from its 1920s' origins as a centre for the then thriving Chapeltown Jewish community.

HOST MEDIA CENTRE
BAUMAN LYONS ARCHITECTS LIMITED

21 Savile Mount, Leeds

Construction Value: £1.95 million
Completion Date: June 2001

Description

Host comprised the conversion and renovation of the former Leeds Trades Club into a media centre containing media-production facilities, offices, conference and training facilities, exhibition space and a café.

History

The building has an intriguing history, stemming from its 1920s' origins as a centre for the then thriving Chapeltown Jewish community. Later, the trade-union movement took the building over as a trades club. For a number of years prior to the commencement of this project, the building lay vacant.

Client's Brief

The concept of the media centre arose from the local community: a thriving, if largely 'underground', music scene led to the idea of a recording studio. This grew to include TV and radio facilities, editing suites, conference facilities, a café and 22 office suites for start-up media businesses. Access to education and training was central to the client's mission. It took some years before a 'cocktail' of funding was realised to enable building work to commence.

Design Process

A design strategy was developed that hinged on a series of issues: impact on townscape, a flow of spaces within the building that avoids intimidating barriers while maintaining adequate security, and making the best use of original features.

The new entrance, overlooking a landscaped car park (a public space used for the start of the city's carnival) is emphasised by a cantilevered balcony and oriel window. Both are angled to the façade, reinforcing the connection back to the city and the institutions that use the centre's facilities. The building is set back some 20 m

from Chapeltown Road, one of the main routes in and out of the city, and is partly screened by an adjacent property. The elevation facing this important route is therefore treated entirely in 'electric blue' as a signifier of its new use and its 'civic-ness', and to create a noticeable contrast for passers-by on Chapeltown Road. The entrance door itself is recessed into a corner and leads to a foyer, with the café on one side and reception straight ahead. In a sense the visitor is in the building 'before they know it', and talking to the receptionist about where they should go.

Accessed from the foyer and visible through a glazed screen is the staircase. Rising the full height of the building, this three-storey slot alongside one of the existing oriel windows is the most dramatic architectural intervention in the building. Inside, varied treatments of the oriels add interest. On the south side, facing the city, they become little balconies, adding unexpected amenity to the office units. On the north side one oriel forms a tea-making area, and the floor is cut back above to give interaction between tea drinkers on both floors.

Once inside the suites and offices, the spaces are essentially cellular and the detailing practical, with some units benefiting from the provision of balconies.

The existing building had fortunately remained watertight, but there were structural issues to be addressed in the build process – there were, for instance, more columns on the top floor than at ground level. Also, the entrance had spawned an ugly brick 1970s extension; its removal allowed the architect to insert the new entrance, which manages to be both effective and subtle – expressing the relationship between old and new, and between city and institution.

The building work started in June 2000, and was completed in June 2001.

144

Project Sign-off

The project is part of the culturally focused regeneration of the city end of Chapeltown Road. It sits alongside the West Indian Centre and Unity Housing Association, both refurbished by the same architectural practice as Host itself. Recent environmental works, again by the same architect, have lifted the design standards of the external street scene.

The Centre reached capacity within the time set out in its business plan, and is standing up well to intensive use. It remains fully occupied, and Host 2 is currently being planned.

The Host Media Centre won a Leeds Award for Architecture Commendation in 2001, and a Civic Trust Commendation Award the following year.

PROJECT TEAM

Client/Building Owner: **Leeds City Council**
Architect: **Bauman Lyons Architects Limited**
Quantity Surveyor: **Bernard Williams Associates**
Structural Engineer: **JSM**
Services Engineer: **Furness Green Partnership**
Main Contractor: **Allenbuild Turner**

145

ALL IMAGES ON THIS SPREAD BY TIM GREEN

KIRKSTALL ABBEY
PURCELL MILLER TRITTON LLP

Kirkstall, Leeds

Construction Value: £2.65 million
Total Project Cost: £4.4 million
Completion Date: Nov 2005

Description
The project was created to restore the abbey ruins and
surrounding landscape and create new visitor facilities in
the lay brothers' reredorter building.

History
The abbey was founded in 1152 by Cistercian monks
from Fountains Abbey. The principal works were
completed *c*.1175 and a storey added to the tower soon
before the Dissolution in 1539. The ruins remain the
most complete Cistercian complex in Britain. They were
gifted to Leeds City Council in 1889.

Client's Brief
Leeds City Council had responsibly maintained the
parkland and ruins for over a century. However by 1999,
the abbey and its grounds required major restoration
works to be undertaken.

The brief was formed by Leeds City Council after
consultation with all parties concerned with the
Scheduled Ancient Monument status of the abbey and
its parkland. The overall aim was to link together, as
a whole project, better parking facilities, the Abbey
House Museum and its new facilities, a new accessible
crossing of the A65, a restored parkland, new visitor,
interpretation and schools facilities in the lay brothers'
reredorter building, and the restored ruins. Accessibility
and lighting were also stressed in the brief so that
traditional uses of the abbey setting for theatrical and
musical events could be sustained and enhanced.

Key technical aspects of the brief were the re-roofing of
the remarkably intact vaulted structures of the north aisle
to prevent leakage and decay, to consider approaches to
the re-flooring of the cloister which is the focus of summer
festival events, to provide full wheelchair access to the nave
of the abbey ruins and ensure sustainability and energy use
in materials specification and services installations.

Design Process
The project was divided into key elements such as the
design for the re-roofing of the nave aisles, the repair,
re-pointing and some replacement of the masonry
fabric of the ruins, the layout and flooring of the cloister,
disabled access particularly to the nave and cloister
and the provision of the visitor centre and school group
facilities. A further significant part of the design process
was the creation and implementation of a landscape
strategy for the site. The fulfilment of the restoration
or creation of these elements of the project was
coordinated by the client team from Leeds City Council
and the lead consultants Purcell Miller Tritton in close
liaison with English Heritage and the range of bodies
concerned with the Scheduled Ancient Monument status
of the abbey and its parkland.

The approach to re-roofing the vaulted spaces of the
abbey was to repair, replace or re-introduce masonry
corbels and supportive string courses at the tops of
walls ready to receive bold, unrefined, CSA certified
timbers. Together, these support roofing of Northumbrian
stone sourced from a precious industry and craft skills
base. The new robust timber structures incorporate a
partial reconstruction of the west front influenced in
design by surviving fragments. The new stone used both
for supporting the roof structures and in the overall
repair works was procured from local sources which
included an original quarry used in 1151. Lime mortars
were used in their most unrefined form.

Whilst the repair and re-pointing work progressed,
invasive vegetation was removed, though surveys of
plant life discovered species of special interest which
were carefully retained.

The response to the cloister element of the project led
to significant changes of layout. Its base was raised

146

by some 600 mm to its original level. By this means, services could be laid above the archaeology of the site and at the same time disabled access to the cloister was created.

This has proved valuable in sustaining and developing the concepts and open air drama programmes which the City Council successfully promotes in the abbey and its grounds. This potential is also enriched by the strip of stone down the nave of the church which creates accessibility, accentuation of the drama of the space and, by unobtrusive inset floor lighting, a remarkable impression of these majestic ruins.

A major objective of the project was to create a new visitor centre for the abbey site with interpretation and school group facilities. These were designed to be complementary to the facilities in the recently restored Abbey House Museum and, through enhanced parking and road crossing arrangements near Abbey House, to form part of a well-connected group of visitor facilities.

The lay brothers' reredorter (medieval toilets!) building had been turned into a well-remembered but basic visitor café. The aim of the new project was to simultaneously present the archaeology of this building and, by a built extension, create modern-day

WCs, interpretation space for the abbey ruins and a base for the management of the abbey, parkland, events and visitor facilities. The response to these requirements was to create a new floor level supported on a steel structure and clear of the original ground level.

An area of the original floor, incorporating the building's drainage channel, has been partly excavated and left exposed. A sensitive treatment of the original roof structure has resulted in its repair, reinforcement and exposure.

The range of facilities require the extension to the medieval building which again has been made with bold simplicity. It is a timber structure in pentice form, roofed in stone slates and with glazed elements to give orientation and views to the abbey and the parkland. The landscape history describes the transition from an abandoned monastic context, through municipal park additions in the Victorian era, to the present restoration of the whole site.

The design approach was to give clear definition to visitor routes, creation of paving, surfacing and tree planting and new accessible connections to the Abbey House Museum and car park. Links were also made to the adjacent Vesper Field open space which was part of the original abbey precinct.

TIM GREEN

TIM GREEN

Project Sign-off

In 1152, the setting of Kirkstall Abbey alongside the River Aire must have seemed similar to that which Fountains or Rievaulx Abbeys still enjoy. In the 18th century it was still sufficiently Romantic to attract the painters of that era, such as Turner, Girtin and Cotman. The soot of the 19th century city remains on the stone of the abbey today.

The whole project for Kirkstall Abbey, through major support from the Heritage Lottery Fund and also from English Heritage and Leeds City Council has resulted in the restoration and representation of a remarkably intact Cistercian site within an urban setting.

PROJECT TEAM

Client/Building Owner: **Leeds City Council**

Architect: **Purcell Miller Tritton LLP**

Project Manager: **Maria Andersson for Davis Langdon**

Quantity Surveyors & Planning Supervisors: **Rex Proctor & Partners**

Structural Engineer: **Capstone Consulting**

Services Engineer: **Lachmann Consultants**

Main Contractor (buildings): **Laing O'Rourke Northern Ltd**

Archaeologists: **Archaeological Services WYAS**

Landscape Contractor: **Leeds City Council Parks & Countryside**

Largely unoccupied and deteriorating for over 20 years, the former brewery comprises a group of substantial stone buildings.

SEAN CONBOY WWW.PHOTO-GENICS.COM

KIRKSTALL BREWERY STUDENT VILLAGE

BOWMAN RILEY ARCHITECTS

Broad Lane, Leeds

Construction Value: £14.75 million
Completion Date: 1997

Description

The conversion of buildings on a landmark Grade II listed former brewery site. The listed structures were converted to study bedrooms and support accommodation, and a further eight new buildings were added.

History

The derelict site housed a group of substantial stone structures, built between 1795 and 1895 with numerous 20th-century alterations and additional buildings. The brewery complex has always been a focal point in the valley, straddling the Leeds and Liverpool Canal and including both a Site of Special Scientific Interest and important woodland.

Client's Brief

Leeds Metropolitan University bought the site to create a significant student village, which would serve their Headingley and Civic Quarter teaching sites but would also avoid the pressure of additional student accommodation within Headingley itself. The village was to establish a secure environment, with flats and leisure facilities accessible to all students.

Design Process

Bowman Riley Architects identified the site's unique potential, matching it to Leeds Metropolitan University's strategic plans to provide high-quality student accommodation within new developments. The site represents one of the most unusual settings for student accommodation in the country: the canalside former brewery includes Grade II listed buildings, the landmark Victorian brick brewing tower, views of the nearby 12th-century Kirkstall Abbey, a protected woodland area and a wetland Site of Special Scientific Interest – all within three miles of the city centre. The stone brewery buildings form the focus of the scheme, providing strong frontages to both Broad Lane and the Leeds

and Liverpool Canal, which divides the site. Largely unoccupied and deteriorating for over 20 years, the former brewery comprises a group of substantial stone buildings. Extraneous structures, plant and canopies were targeted for demolition, in order to allow the original masonry buildings to be reused. To fully utilise these structures, it was decided that the canalside warehouse would be occupied by student flats with the remaining buildings used for all the ancillary accommodation, thus providing a buffer to the noisy public highway.

While maintaining the original buildings, it was always felt that the passage of time and change of use of this complex should not be eradicated. Therefore, the cleaning and reconstruction exercises were undertaken in such a way that the scars of time were not totally obliterated: the outline of later structures can still be identified, for example, as can the repair of façades or, in some places, the different materials employed over the centuries.

To maximise the use of the site in the vicinity of these existing buildings a large area was excavated adjacent to the former warehouse, which enabled the subterranean level of this structure to be brought into beneficial use. In addition, substantial openings (at level 2) required re-walling while numerous semicircular-headed windows were repaired and/or reinstalled.

The project provides 1,018 study bedrooms within 180 flats, with a further six units for residential site offices. The car-parking provision was limited to approximately one space per flat. As a student-centred pedestrian environment, the village is provided with necessary but controlled vehicle access. Eight new buildings sit upon the steeply terraced landscaped site and along both sides of the canal, overlooking the valley and the ruins of Kirkstall Abbey. Of these new structures, 80 per cent

150

BOWMAN RILEY ARCHITECTS

are faced in stone and have slate roofs. The new buildings on the western site boundary sit adjacent to existing brick housing, and are themselves brick-clad. A new timber footbridge above the canal and its towpath unites the two elements of the site, old and new. Nearly 1.2 hectares of the site are occupied by protected woodland with natural springs – and this area provides a valuable amenity for the whole scheme.

Planning approval was obtained in 1994, with a Design and Build contract commencing in 1995 (the architect was novated). The project was delivered in three phases utilising traditional construction methods, with completion in 1997.

Project Sign-off

The project shows that it is possible to revitalise derelict sites and return listed buildings to beneficial use – and introduce a number of new buildings – without diminishing the status of existing buildings or destroying their historical setting. Indeed, for the students who now call Kirkstall Brewery home the sense of the valley's history is never far away. The names of the new residences, such as 'Musgrave' and 'Cooper', add a further resonance of times past: it was in the late 18th century that Joseph Musgrave and Henry Cooper first built maltings on this site. Three decades later, the great English watercolourist J. M. W. Turner sat where students' homes now stand – among them, Turner House – and painted his view of Kirkstall Lock and the River Aire. Kirkstall Brewery has a long and interesting history, but that has been in no way compromised by the establishment of a student village with modern buildings that has simply added another chapter to the valley's history.

SEAN CONROY WWW.PHOTO-GENICS.COM

PROJECT TEAM

Client/Building Owner: **Leeds Metropolitan University**
Architect: **Bowman Riley Architects**
Quantity Surveyor: **Hayes Thornber Walker**
Structural Engineer: **Curtins**
Services Engineer: **Elequip**
Main Contractor: **Morrison Construction Limited**

PARK LANE COLLEGE EXTENSION

ALLEN TOD ARCHITECTURE LIMITED

Park Lane, Leeds

Construction Value: £7 million
Completion Date: autumn 2004

Description

A low-energy new-build extension to an existing further education college, comprising additional flexible teaching space and a new entrance offering universal access and improved visibility.

History

Park Lane College's main building was built in the 1970s. In 2002, the college commissioned Allen Tod Architecture to investigate the long-term potential of their main city-centre site in the context of their wider estate and plans for the future.

Client's Brief

The architects' masterplan, designed in response to the brief, addressed the college's demand for more space on a central campus with enhanced environmental performance, better circulation, improved accessibility and a more prominent image.

The project represents the first phase of this masterplan, comprising a seven-storey block housing teaching space for A-level courses and a new entrance building that improves the visibility and identity of the college as well as upgrading accessibility and security.

Design Process

The design was driven by a commitment to produce premises that are energy-efficient, and has resulted in two striking buildings with a simple form and a distinctive palette of materials.

The building is orientated with teaching-room windows on its east and west elevations. This reduces the impact of solar gain to the south elevation and mitigates the impact of traffic noise from Park Lane, a busy artery into the city.

The ground floors are constructed of polished concrete blockwork, which creates a solid base for both buildings.

Above the ground floor, the elevations have a timber rainscreen cladding made from renewable sources. The cladding includes timber louvres to the windows that further help to control solar gain to the buildings and reduce the need for cooling plant.

The top floor is finished in Kalwall, a semi-transparent insulated-panel system, creating a translucent, glowing box at the top of the building.

The south elevation of Building A is clad in photovoltaic panels, which capitalise on the orientation of the building and provide up to 15 per cent of its electrical energy requirements.

Both structures are designed with high levels of insulation. Building A has exposed concrete ceilings that provide a high thermal mass, helping to stabilise the temperature of the building and place less demand on heating and cooling plant.

The roofs have a planted sedum finish that contributes to insulation levels, absorbs CO_2 and mitigates rainwater run-off. The college site sits adjacent to a Conservation Area. The scale of the project required detailed negotiations with planning and conservation officers, and a clear demonstration of the impact of the development on the Conservation Area. As a result of the negotiations, the top storey of Building A was set back to reduce its perceived impact upon the adjacent square and the Kalwall cladding was introduced on the top floor in lieu of timber.

The building was required to be completed in time for the start of the Autumn 2004 academic year. The planning application was submitted in November 2002,

with approval being granted the following February. Construction work started on site in July 2003, and the client was able to move in to their new premises in September of 2004.

Project Sign-off

This new development improves and expands the facilities of an important social resource on Park Lane College's city-centre site. The new buildings allow the college to consolidate more services on this central site, a strategy which offers logistical and ecological advantages.

The project recognises its urban setting and its proximity to historical spaces but also looks forward, as an unmistakably modern building, with high aspirations for good future energy performance.

PROJECT TEAM

Client/Building Owner: **Park Lane College**
Architect: **Allen Tod Architecture Limited**
Quantity Surveyor: **EC Harris**
Structural Engineer: **Jacobs**
Services Engineer: **Halcrow**
Main Contractor: **Allenbuild**

153

East Street Arts (ESA) is a small, not-for-profit studio group delivering events, advocacy, space and training for visual artists.

PATRICK STUDIOS
BAUMAN LYONS ARCHITECTS LIMITED

St Mary's Lane, Leeds

Construction Value: £1.04 million
Completion Date: May 2004

Description

The conversion and restoration of a former church social club on the outskirts of the city centre into artists' studios and support facilities.

History

The building is situated between the northeast edge of the city centre and the neighbouring inner-city communities of Ebor Gardens, Burmantofts and Harehills. The premises were built in 1905 to house the St Patrick's Roman Catholic Church Social Club, on a tight site which was originally the courtyard to St Patrick's Church.

Client's Brief

East Street Arts (ESA) is a small, not-for-profit studio group delivering events, advocacy, space and training for visual artists. It has managed studio-based spaces in Leeds for over ten years, largely in semi-derelict buildings that did not meet basic health-and-safety or access requirements.

ESA wanted to create a new visual arts centre to house a mix of artists and other creative practitioners. The building was also to accommodate arts resources and facilities, and provide a space for events and exhibitions to serve not only the needs of individual artists but also the local community and wider public.

Design Process

Design proposals were developed in close consultation with the client. The design brief evolved as information was gathered through market research into artists' requirements, changing artist practice, case studies and the practical restraints of the existing building and of the budget available for the conversion.

In their design proposals Bauman Lyons responded to the client's wishes for a robust, honest building,

which would be unpretentious and would avoid being dominated by an inappropriate desire to make an architectural 'statement'. Notwithstanding this, the existing building held a range of architectural opportunities in its large volumes, regular high-window patterns, strong timber roof trusses and the quality of its existing materials, such as the brickwork and floorboards. Wherever possible, therefore, the existing features of the building have been utilised to enhance the new spaces, and the surfaces have been left intentionally raw to reveal the building's history. The L-shaped building had a relatively simple internal layout at ground and first floors, but became more complicated thereafter because of an existing stage at one end of its large north–south wing on the first floor. The volume occupied by the auditorium in the main building meant that there were two additional floors in the east–west wing.

The development of this upper level warranted particular attention. The raised stage area was removed, and a new floor inserted which continued the auditorium floor along the full length of the building. This created a large double-height volume. At the northern end, this volume was left uninterrupted, in order to form a large project space for exhibitions. The remainder of the space was divided with a mezzanine level. This new half-level is essentially a 'box' sitting within the roof space and supported on new twinned steel beams, which rest on the wall below the bosses of the original roof trusses. The box is set in by around 2.5 m from the external walls, and extends up to the underside of the roof. The mezzanine level itself is lit by new rooflights, and forms an open-plan shared workspace with artists' workstations. This device of spacing the new construction back off the external walls means that the existing windows are allowed to remain uninterrupted. These windows, together with a series of rooflights and

the large expanse of white wall to the mezzanine above, give each of the studios on this level a double-height section infused with light.

A new steel-and-Douglas-fir staircase and a lift cut through the building, creating social and circulation space at the heart of the project. A new entrance area and doorway have been formed by cutting down an existing window reveal to street level in order to allow full access. All existing wooden openings and features are restored and painted in their original colours; all new openings are framed in Douglas fir and aluminium.

The building work started in August 2003 and was completed in May 2004.

Project Sign-off

Patrick Studios brings an added dimension to the emerging creative-arts 'hub' that is developing in the immediate locality. In particular, it adds a visual-arts element to existing cultural activity already underway or planned by the West Yorkshire Playhouse, the Yorkshire Dance Centre, Leeds College of Music, and Northern Ballet and Phoenix Dance.

The project contributes to the overall economic regeneration of the neighbourhood in which the studio space is located through its positive impact on the built environment, as well as its work to create increased wealth in the sector. Above all, Patrick Studios gives a home and focus to emerging artists in Leeds, encouraging them to stay and contribute towards the city's future.

MARTINE HAMILTON KNIGHT

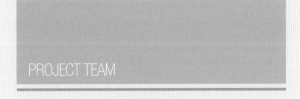

PROJECT TEAM

Client/Building Owner: **East Street Arts**
Architect: **Bauman Lyons Architects Limited**
Quantity Surveyor: **Bernard Williams Associates**
Structural Engineer: **Buro Happold**
Services Engineer: **Furness Green Partnership**
Main Contractor: **Vincent Dobson (Builders) Limited**

155

> The plan of the extension is a composition of layered planes that suggest 'rooms within rooms' – a device used by certain architects belonging to the early 20th-century Arts and Crafts movement.

WETHERBY HOUSE

OMI ARCHITECTS

Wetherby, Leeds

Construction Value: undisclosed
Completion Date: January 2003

Description

Additions and alterations to an existing house and garden in the outlying town of Wetherby.

History

The existing Georgian house sits within a tight row of villas in a Conservation Area in the centre of town. The house backs directly onto the river, and its walled-garden setting is typical of the local vernacular.

Client's Brief

The client expressed a desire for a 'liveable', minimal aesthetic which offered a relaxed, open arrangement in contrast to the formal rooms and more enclosed quality of the existing house.

Design Process

The hard street frontage to the existing dwelling provides only hints of the Modernist intervention behind, which cascades down the rear garden towards the river and overlooks the plain beyond.

The main focus of the additions is a new living room with large areas of retractable glazing which allow the internal space to 'crack open' at the corner, exploiting views out to a bend in the river.

The plan of the extension is a composition of layered planes that suggest 'rooms within rooms' – a device used by certain architects belonging to the early 20th-century Arts and Crafts movement.

The restricted palette of materials for the new additions aims to complement the mellow brick and stone of the existing house – using new local limestone, untreated oak, through-coloured render and grey-painted steel.

These new forms and materials are extended into the garden in order to reinforce the connection between the

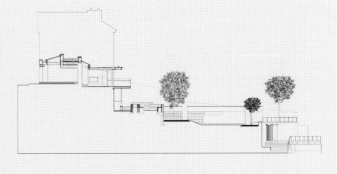

house and its setting, in a tiered sequence of terraces and walls leading down to the river.

Project Sign-off

In the architects' view, this project represents a form of contemporary architecture which draws inspiration from its context.

OMI have tried to connect with the 'spirit' of the existing building, as opposed to directly reproducing its outward characteristics.

This reinterpretation has allowed the clients a new experience of living in their house, making strong connections to the garden and the river in a way which would otherwise not have been possible.

PROJECT TEAM

Client/Building Owner: **Undisclosed**
Architect: **OMI Architects**
Quantity Surveyor: **Harvey and Company**
Structural Engineer: **Woolgar Hunter**
Services Engineer: **John Troughear**
Main Contractor: **Maysand**
Specialist Joinery: **Carey and Greenslade Compass Interiors**

THE MARTIN HOUSE CHAPEL BOSTON SPA
WILDBLOOD MACDONALD

Grove Road, Boston Spa, Leeds

Construction Value: £110 thousand
Completion Date: summer 2002

Description

A new chapel, to replace an earlier one built in 1987, was required to enable the construction of a new teenage unit for the hospice.

History

From the opening of Martin House Children's Hospice in 1987, there had been a vision of constructing a young persons' hospice to work alongside the facility for younger children. The opportunity arose in 2000 when Whitby Lodge, a residential building within the grounds, became available for conversion. However, this entailed the loss of the hospice's chapel, and, as a consequence, a replacement was required.

Client's Brief

The governors of Martin House simply asked Wildblood Macdonald to design a new, replacement chapel somewhere within the grounds. The architects were asked to replicate the ethos of the original chapel, and to incorporate a number of fixtures that had been donated over the years by benefactors.

Design Process

Leeds played a major role in the creation of Martin House some 25 years ago. Paediatricians from the Leeds teaching hospitals were amongst those who strove to found a children's hospice in the North of England.

Located 12 miles from the city centre – on the narrow strip of magnesian limestone that runs either side of the A1 'Great North Road', and at the edge of Boston Spa village – Martin House owes little to the built form of Leeds. Rather, its design seeks to contrast with the city and relate closely to the domestic qualities of the village.

Only the second children's hospice in Western Europe, Martin House opened its doors to children with life-threatening illnesses and their families in July 1987. It comprised two buildings: the main hospice and a residential home for an order of nuns, who in the early years played their part in the care of the children. The hospice chapel was at the heart of their home.

The nuns decided in 1999 to vacate this property, and through its conversion to facilitate the creation of a Young Persons' Unit. This had been the vision of a number of the governors and staff from the opening in 1987, but the decision to convert and extend the Sisters' residence clearly had repercussions for its chapel. All concerned agreed that a noisy location at the heart of the teenagers' home was not ideal for a place of meditation and prayer. A decision was taken to construct a new building in the garden.

The agreed setting, and the fact that the garden lay within the Green Belt, led the architects to conclude that the building should blend into the landscape, with any walls appearing as garden walls.

This led Wildblood Macdonald on to think that they should make positive use of the 'boundary wall' idea. They concluded that those visiting the chapel should walk through the wall to something delightful beyond. For some this would represent a step from the bustling activity of the hospice to a quiet garden setting, but for others it could symbolise the passing from life, through death, to a life full of delight beyond.

The use of dry-stone walling as a facing for the wall adds emphasis to this concept, provides a contrast with the extensive use of timber in the chapel itself and brings to the building something of Yorkshire tradition.

Of great importance to the designers was the use of a glass entrance door through the wall. This dispels any bunker-like qualities that the building might otherwise have had, and gives glimpses of what lies ahead.

158

The design of the chapel also reflects the wish of all involved for some continuity with its predecessor. An aumbry has been brought over and walled in to the dry-stone wall. The stained-glass cross originally forming the reredos to the altar has been adapted and built into the glazed screen wall of the new building, and the large external cross follows the design of its predecessor.

Project Sign-off

Although Martin House and its chapel are remote from the bustle of Leeds city centre, they play a significant role in its life. Martin House is meant to be a holiday destination, school and a home rolled into one. It fulfils this role for a considerable number of families from Leeds as well as for others from further afield in the North of England.

Martin House works very closely with the specialist units in the Leeds teaching hospitals, and it provides an element to the care of children additional to that which they are able to offer.

As for its buildings, in purely architectural terms they contribute to the wide palette of good design to be found within the city's administrative area.

PROJECT TEAM

Client/Building Owner: **The Governors of Martin House**
Architect: **Wildblood Macdonald**
Quantity Surveyor: **MHB Partnership**
Structural Engineer: **Robert T Horne and Partners**
Main Contractor: **Lemmeleg**

161

CONTEXTUAL LEEDS

What makes a city, a city? Or to put the
question another way, what makes Leeds,
Leeds? The monuments which historically
have given the city its identity have changed
with almost every generation.

Yet what one generation hoped to express with the
Town Hall was no different to what another did with the
Headrow. Thus it is all the more surprising that it was
the same inter-war years which gave Leeds its most
famous thoroughfare that also saw the construction
of the vast Quarry Hill housing estate designed by the
City Architects' Department (headed by R. A. H. Livett)
in 1935. This socialist gesture, accommodating over
3,000 people in the manner of Berlin and Viennese
apartment blocks, has been swept away and replaced,
ironically, by Quarry House, initially the home of the
DHSS, the government department then responsible for
the distribution of social benefits.

> Quarry Hill flats
in the 1940s
ENGLISH HERITAGE/
AEROFILMS ARCHIVE

> Quarry House,
the National
Health Service
headquarters
WWW.JH-JPHOTO.CO.UK

^ Former Bank of England
South Parade
WWW.JH-JPHOTO.CO.UK

^ Local Burmantofts
faience on the
Metropole Hotel
WWW.JH-JPHOTO.CO.UK

All development is cyclical, and it now seems that
Leeds is emerging into a new 'spring'. The mistakes (to
some) of Quarry House and the ubiquitous 'Leeds Look'
are of the past, and a bright future is beckoning –
whether that be the sleek, glass façades of 15/16 Park
Row, designed by careyjones architects; or the more
tactile, prefabricated forms of the CASPAR housing
scheme by Levitt Bernstein. In the same way that the
millstone grit of the early 19th century, and the red
brick and terracotta of the later 1800s, gave way to
the brick and Portland stone of the early 20th century,
so the concrete of the post-war developments is now
giving way to a Modernist, tectonic aesthetic which will
signify 'Leeds' for years to come.

< The former central
Post Office,
now restaurants
and apartments
overlooking City
Square
WWW.JH-JPHOTO.CO.UK

^ The Electric
Press building and
Carriageworks
Theatre, Millennium
Square
WWW.JH-JPHOTO.CO.UK

The old city is slowly altering its appearance, and
with it the nature of its street life. What was the Bank
of England on South Parade, built by Philip Hardwick
in 1864, has become a sports bar. Similarly, the old
Midland Bank on City Square, a domed and columned
corner building of 1899 by W. W. Gwyther, is now a
nightclub; while, across the square, the former General
Post Office of 1896, designed by Sir Henry Tanner,
has been converted into restaurants and smart hotel
apartments. In front of E. Vincent Harris's Civic Hall of
1933 the new Millennium Square has been created,
and the old Electric Press Building and Stansfeld
Chambers opposite provide a new cultural focus for
the city.

The lack of major new 'object buildings' or iconic
architecture is perhaps what distinguishes Leeds
most from its northern rivals such as Manchester and
Newcastle-upon-Tyne. Leeds' iconic buildings are of
the 19th century; modern Leeds, Contextual Leeds, is
a city of organic change, where infill developments and
changes of use serve to knit the city together and allow
it to grow outwards, once again, from the centre.

15–16 PARK ROW

CAREYJONES ARCHITECTS

15–16 Park Row, Leeds

Construction Value: £3.5 million
Completion Date: February 1997

Description

A speculative office development on an infill site on Park Row. This new-build scheme replaced a highly inefficient office building constructed in the 1960s.

History

Historically, Park Row was the principal banking/financial street in the city; it effectively joins the Civic Quarter to City Square and the railway station. The thoroughfare comprises many fine buildings, from the listed 'Bank of England' to the 1980s Lloyds Bank, and includes a Waterhouse-designed Prudential building. Much of its architecture represents the finest craftsmanship and technology of the time.

Client's Brief

Scottish Mutual ran an invited competition for design ideas, with three main intentions. First, they wanted an efficient commercial building that maximised lettable floor area within the confines of the site and neighbouring properties. Second, they wished to improve the site's built presence on Park Row; and finally, they needed a flexible design to allow for either single or multiple occupancy.

Design Process

Upon winning the competition, two primary objectives formed the basis of careyjones' ideas for this project: to achieve an efficient office floorplate on such a restrictive site, and to achieve a contextual response to the many fine 19th-century banking/financial buildings facing onto Park Row.

The 1960s commercial building that occupied the site, demolished as part of the contract, was of poor visual quality and inefficient in plan, with a central core effectively cutting its floorplate in two and producing a layout that was highly restrictive for modern office usage.

The design had to reconcile an existing lightwell to the adjoining property, and form new street frontages to Park Row and Upper Basinghall Street.

The architects' solution was to develop an open floorplate, taking advantage of daylight from the adjoining lightwell and pushing the circulation cores to diagonally opposing corners of the building. This provided a clear, uncluttered office floorplate with good natural daylight from the two street frontages and the central lightwell. The two cores were arranged to give the necessary interconnection between floor levels as well as providing the required escape routes from all parts of the building.

In evolving their ideas for the principal frontages of the scheme, careyjones were acutely aware of the fine architecture and craftsmanship of the 19th-century buildings facing Park Row, and came to an early conclusion that a pastiche option was not the route to follow for two reasons: first, the desire to be innovative and break the 'Leeds Look' syndrome which was prevalent at the time of the competition; second, it would be an unreasonable expectation to match the quality of detail of the 19th-century stonework and terracotta with contemporary skills and materials.

Their approach, therefore, was to adopt their civic forebears' ethics in demanding the best from the technology of the time, and to translate this into a late-20th-century piece of contemporary architecture. Running in parallel with these thoughts were considerations of traffic noise from, and yet the requirement to achieve a principal entrance off, Park Row.

The solution was a double-façade treatment to Park Row, with the office floorplate cut back from the main building line and the adoption of a structural-glass

166

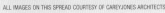
ALL IMAGES ON THIS SPREAD COURTESY OF CAREYJONES ARCHITECTS

façade to the outer face. This achieved the primary objectives in assimilating modern technology into the proposals and creating a dramatic entrance – formed by an atrium running the full height of the building on the Park Lane frontage – whilst also resolving any traffic-noise issues.

The Park Row elevation was arranged with paired 'bookends' – formed from two-tone Karin grey granite with stainless-steel inserts – with the striking, suspended structural-glass face running between. The composition is further enhanced by the articulation of the circulation core, with the main lift lobbies opening up onto the atrium space and the granite being taken from outside to inside, expressing this feature.

Scottish Mutual appointed careyjones architects to carry out the project, and the scheme was duly submitted to Leeds City Council for a full planning consent. The application was well received by the council, who viewed it as a step change in quality and architecture at the time, and planning approval was granted in July 1994.

Project Sign-off

A site start was made in August 1995, with completion reached in February 1997.

The completed project marked a significant point in the history of Leeds architecture. Although one of the later non-'Leeds Look' developments by the time it was completed, the initial scheme did effectively set new directions in architectural style. The completed building achieves a high standard of design in a truly contemporary manner which is enhanced by the attention to detail, choice of materials and execution. This, together with its use of technology, illustrates a positive and confident

approach to replacing the city's buildings and helped set new benchmarks for design of commercial buildings in the centre.

The visual qualities of the building are further enhanced by a 'kaleidoscope' lighting scheme, utilising fibre optics integrated into the structural-glass-wall steel supports. The lighting adds a further design dimension at night, for which the building received a Leeds Lighting Award.

PROJECT TEAM

Client: **Scottish Mutual Assurance plc**
Building Owner: **PRUPRIM**
Architect: **careyjones architects**
Quantity Surveyor: **Bucknall Austin**
Structural Engineer: **Buro Happold**
Services Engineer: **Buro Happold**
Main Contractor: **Shepherd Construction Limited**
Steelwork Fabricator: **Monkbridge Construction Limited**
Façade Engineer: **MAG Design and Build**
Glazing System: **MAG Design and Build**

The project is located in a Conservation Area,
and addresses the Grade I listed Corn Exchange
of 1863 by Cuthbert Brodrick.

CROWN STREET BUILDINGS
ALLFORD HALL MONAGHAN MORRIS LLP ARCHITECTS

31–33 Call Lane, Leeds

Construction Value: £6.1 million
Completion Date: August 2005

Description

Crown Street Buildings is a major mixed-use project
in the Exchange Quarter of Leeds. It comprises 57
apartments above a base of commercial units.

History

The project is located in a Conservation Area, and
addresses the Grade I listed Corn Exchange of 1863
by Cuthbert Brodrick. It occupies a complex triangular
site that has long been vacant, bounded on its other
two sides by a railway viaduct and existing Victorian
commercial buildings which are integrated into the
scheme.

Client's Brief

The client's brief for the original design competition was
for a striking, contemporary and efficient mixed-use
building on this difficult and historically sensitive city-
centre site.

Design Process

The design of this project has to respond to and address
very different conditions on the three sides of its
roughly triangular site. To the north the inflected curve
of its long elevation addresses, and is subordinate to,
the powerful curved form of the Corn Exchange. The
southwest elevation to Call Lane – a busy commercial
thoroughfare – consists predominantly of a refurbished
terrace of robust Victorian commercial buildings. Finally,
to the south the building addresses the elevated railway
viaduct, and the new flats here look out over the viaduct
to the landscape beyond.

The commission was secured after a limited design
competition in 2001. The requirements of the city
planners and the Civic Architect – for a high-quality
scheme, modern whilst respecting its Victorian context
– were paramount. Indeed, the project would not have

TIM SOAR

BOTH IMAGES ON THIS PAGE TIM SOAR

been realised without the close cooperation and support of these parties – in particular the Leeds Civic Architect, John Thorp.

To respond to these considerations, the elevations employ the predominant 19th-century warehouse type as a model. A brick skin of traditional pressed Victorian-style bricks is perforated with large, deep openings mirroring the structural frame behind. These openings are infilled with aluminium windows and glazed faience panels, and the treatment of their deep reveals reflects the fact that the building is mainly experienced in oblique view. The panels take their cue from the coloured faience examples found throughout Leeds, especially in its arcades, and there is a graduated change in colour from blue, on the Call Lane corner; through green, at the eastern end of the long elevation; to yellow, on the viaduct elevation. The apartment layouts are handed on alternate floors so that these panels, which are of essentially two types to respond to the bedroom and living-room conditions, stagger and offset to provide the elevation with a dynamic rhythm.

The flats are planned to minimise internal circulation and to maximise usable area. This is made possible by providing a secondary means of escape through the second bedroom. The apartments are accessed off walkways that line the private internal courtyard at first-floor level, over the commercial units below.

There is no parking associated with these flats – this was a specific planning requirement.

Working within a constrained budget, the design carefully allocated the available resources to ensure that they went

to the areas where the building's civic qualities would be best displayed. A decision was made to ensure that the external façade was of an appropriate material to 'empathise' with its historical surroundings. The faience material (glazed basalt) was critical to the success of the design, given its prominence on the building. In order to make this possible, a simpler render was chosen for the internal courtyard. This cool, white finish, with galvanised metalwork, contrasts with the street façade and gives the raised private internal courtyard a very different feel from the external elevations. The intention was to create an outdoor 'room' within the city.

Project Sign-off

The building anchors the southeastern corner of Leeds' central retail district, and has refocused this area of the city centre whilst acting, at the same time, as a link through to the neighbouring residential Calls district.

The project has been recognised with a Housing Design Awards 'Project' Award in 2001, followed by a full 'Completed Project' Award in 2006. The City of Leeds itself has also, in 2007, awarded the project one of two Leeds Architecture Awards for the best completed schemes within the city.

TIM SOAR

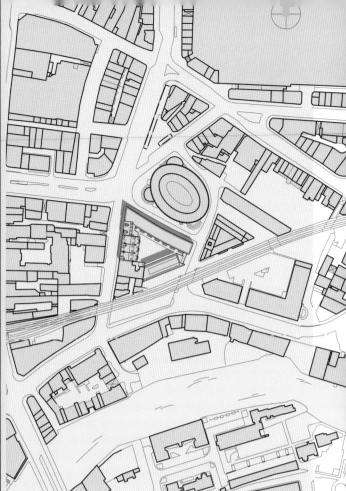

ALLFORD HALL MONAGHAN MORRIS

TIM SOAR

Client/Building Owner: **Welfield Limited**

Architect: **Allford Hall Monaghan Morris LLP Architects**

Quantity Surveyor: **Murdoch Green Kensalls**

Structural Engineer: **Peter Brett Associates**

Services Engineer: **Cameron Taylor Brady**

Main Contractor: **Allenbuild North East**

Environmental Engineer: **Peter Brett Associates**

173

Since it was located in the Riverside Conservation Area, and had no land onto which to expand, the designers focused on the riverside elevation for architectural interest and expression.

LEEDS DESIGN INNOVATION CENTRE

ALLEN TOD ARCHITECTURE LIMITED

44–46 The Calls, Leeds

Construction Value: £650 thousand
Completion Date: April 1988

Description

The Design Innovation Centre involved the conversion and alteration of a three-storey grain warehouse on the River Aire to form studio offices and a gallery.

History

The warehouse was built around 1930 in red engineering brick, with a steel frame, in situ concrete-and-asphalt flat roof, and composite timber floors. It stood alone, with a cleared site on one side and a builder's yard on the other. It has no curtilage beyond the building footprint, and is tightly situated between The Calls, a narrow cobbled street, and the river.

Client's Brief

Peter Connolly, together with Nick Allen and Ian Tod of Allen Tod Architecture formed Yorkshire Design Services Limited and acquired the building in 1986, aiming to develop what was then a pioneering managed-workspace project for design-related businesses – hence the gallery space as 'showroom'. They wrote their own brief, focusing on the design quality of the common areas, flexibility, and providing every office with a balcony over the water – all within a very tight budget.

Design Process

As a pioneering private-sector regeneration project in a run-down, blighted area of Leeds, the building had to be made attractive to prospective tenants. Since it was located in the Riverside Conservation Area, and had no land onto which to expand, the designers focused on the riverside elevation for architectural interest and expression. As a 1930s warehouse the building had none of the Victorian industrial character prevalent elsewhere in the city, presenting instead very bland, red-brick façades beneath a flat roof.

Allen Tod's approach was based around the building's existing 'lucams', or hoist towers: they stripped off their cladding, suspended another floor below the existing structure and clad these in glass – creating meeting rooms projecting out over the river.

Every office was given a balcony built in zinc-finished steel, with a handrail designed to stand drinks glasses on. Internally, a large central atrium and stairwell with lift was formed, giving access to all the units via generous corridors which were widened to give a sense of 'entrance' to each unit.

A major obstacle arose early on, in that Leeds City Council had zoned the area as 'light industrial' and were not keen on the idea of office use. They also wanted off-street tenants' parking, and suggested that this be located on the ground floor – a move that would have rendered the whole project unviable. However, the officers were overruled on both counts by elected members, who had been persuaded by Allen Tod's conviction that such narrow zoning was not relevant, that 'mixed-use' meant 'mixed', and that studio offices would help regenerate the area; and additionally, as a city-centre site, the development should not encourage car use and would, indeed, be viable with minimal parking.

In addition, the council had at that time plans for a riverside walkway, and insisted on a full-length balcony at ground-floor level. This had to be suspended from the lucams to avoid introducing any structure below the deck that might cause obstruction during floods. The riverside walkway, however, was never built, leaving the balcony unconnected to anything, but an asset to the tenants.

No special methods of construction were used in the project, other than the steel-cable

suspension of the main balcony and the lower floors of the three lucams. The maple-finished softwood floors

175

were simply sanded and sealed, and all internal partitions were built in timber stud to enable local builders to easily move them – something which has since successfully been done on a number of occasions.

Work was begun on site in mid-1987, and took nine months with no particular problems or cost overruns.

Project Sign-off

This was undoubtedly a very significant project in the regeneration of the Leeds riverside, which, in the mid-1980s, had been virtually ignored.

Architecturally, it helped break the mould of the infamous and frustrating 'Leeds Look' – introducing steel, glass and colour in a way that transformed a drab red-brick building into an exciting and attractive piece of architecture.

More importantly, it pointed the way for developers to exploit other run-down riverside warehouses, and led directly to other developments – notably, the refurbishment of 32 The Calls for residential and leisure use; 42 The Calls, now a famous hotel and restaurant; and The Chandlers, again for residential use; together with extensive new-build waterside residential developments. The momentum generated by these projects spread rapidly to the regeneration of the south side of the river, as well as to the areas between The Calls and the city centre.

ALL THE IMAGES ON THIS SPREAD WWW.JH-JPHOTO.CO.UK

PROJECT TEAM

Client/Building Owner: **Yorkshire Design Services Limited**
Architect: **Allen Tod Architecture Limited**
Quantity Surveyor: **BWA**
Structural Engineer: **Michael Heal**
Main Contractor: **Harrisons**

Seen from outside, the building has a robust
form which responds to the 19th-century
converted warehouses that line this section
of the river.

NO. 1 DOCK STREET
CAREYJONES ARCHITECTS

No. 1 Dock Street, Leeds

Construction Value: £5.5 million
Completion Date: September 2002

Description

The building is the new-build element of the No.1 Dock
Street development by Wilson Connolly (now owned by
Taylor Wimpey).

History

The development is located in central Leeds on the south
bank of the River Aire, close to Leeds Bridge. The site
was formerly occupied by warehouses of varying age
and quality, including the former Aire & Calder Navigation
Headquarters building.

Client's Brief

Wilson Connolly's brief was to maximise the
accommodation within the scheme whilst treating
the new-build component of the development in an
architecturally sympathetic manner. The new-build multi-
storey element was to be constructed on what was
formerly the staff car park of the Aire & Calder Navigation
Headquarters building.

Design Process

The new building is set within a Conservation Area, with
surrounding listed buildings. It houses 51 apartments
within a six-storey block, which completes one side of a
garden space partly contained by the existing buildings.
The planning consent included the refurbishment and
conversion of No. 1 Dock Street and the refurbishment
of Bridge End and Simpson's Fold (both listed buildings),
giving an overall total of 94 flats.

Seen from outside, the building has a robust form which
responds to the 19th-century converted warehouses that
line this section of the river. Its faceted elevations follow
both the bend in the river and the curve of Navigation
Walk, allowing the building to fit the site with a unified
'expression'.

The set-back top floor, with its projecting roof, provides a
key element of lightness in contrast to the heavy stonework
below, with the roof appearing to float above the main
structure.

The sandstone ashlar cladding is given texture and scale
through alternating course-depths and shadow joints.
Bespoke iroko-framed windows add a further layer of depth
and warmth to the elevations. Within the plot, a new court is
formed between the new and existing buildings. The siting
of the building allows views into this landscaped courtyard,
whilst maintaining vistas of the river.

The new building courtyard elevations are given a lighter
treatment than the external façades, with larger areas
of glazing and cream render walls both admitting and
reflecting the maximum possible amount of light.

Car parking for the development is located in the courtyard
and below the new structure. To mask this, and to provide
amenity space for the residents, a timber access deck is
formed above, incorporating a projecting viewing platform
which cantilevers out over the river. Planted line wires
are fixed between this deck and the buildings, so that the
apparent floor of the court will be a mass of greenery,
without compromising the levels of natural light and
ventilation to the parking below. A publicly accessible
riverside terrace includes seating and tree planting.

The apartments are arranged around a single core and a
curving corridor. Variations in ceiling heights give definition
and interest to the principal rooms. Finishes include
full-height, large-format tiling to bathrooms and granite
surfaces to kitchens. The upper floors have continuous roof
terraces to the perimeter, with full-height glazing to the
duplex units behind.

While the original brief was written in 1997, the project
did not start on site until June 2001 and the work was

completed in September 2002. The contract was Design and Build, for a £5.5 million development over a 56-week construction period.

Project Sign-off

No. 1 Dock Street has added significantly to the continuing development of the centre of Leeds along the banks of the River Aire. The project provides a striking external façade, which also has a positive relationship with the surrounding listed buildings. The architects have produced an exciting and innovative scheme on what is an important site. The scheme won a City of Leeds Architecture Award in 2000.

PROJECT TEAM

Client/Building Owner: **Wilson Connolly Homes**
Architect: **careyjones architects**
Quantity Surveyor: **Richard Boothroyd & Associates**
Services Engineer: **Wheatley**
Main Contractor: **Miller Construction**
Acoustic Consultant: **BDP Acoustic**
Landscape Consultant: **Donaldson Edwards Partnership**

The existing steel-framed structure
of the 1960s building required
modification and strengthening in part,
with the original atrium to the shopping
arcade being infilled, leaving only the
smaller escalator-atrium passing full-
height through the store.

HARVEY NICHOLS

BROOKER FLYNN ARCHITECTS

107–111 Briggate, Leeds

Construction Value: £9 million
Completion Date: October 1996

Description

The conversion of a 1960s infill office block within an existing Victorian arcade into a high-quality retail outlet.

History

The development is on Briggate, a main shopping street in Leeds city centre. Originally the site of the exuberant Empire Theatre, it forms part of the specialist Victorian shopping arcades known as The Victoria Quarter. The theatre was eventually replaced in the 1960s by an office building, Empire House, and the Empire Shopping Arcade, which now forms the basis for the Harvey Nichols store.

Client's Brief

The client, with Leeds as their first outlet outside London, required the Harvey Nichols ethos to be embodied in their new building and to become a catalyst for further regional expansion. The store was to trade on four floors, offering a wide variety of retail and catering options.

Design Process

Interior designers Hosker Moore and Kent were appointed to develop the concept for the building and the interior fit-out, with a brief to recreate the ambience of Harvey Nichols' Knightsbridge store. They proposed a dramatic four-storey-high planar glass frontage, with internal atrium, to replace the exposed concrete framing of the existing 1960s building, thus providing a modern design statement, giving enticing views into the store and acting as a foil to the neighbouring Victorian façades.

Brooker Flynn Architects were appointed to progress the conceptual design. Working closely with Leeds City Council planners and building inspectors, together with English Heritage, it was essential to retain as much as possible of the Grade II listed façades and interiors of the Victorian units on Briggate, Queen Victoria Street and Cross Arcade. The façades were cleaned, repaired

and refurbished. New piers were added to the Briggate elevation, sympathetic to the original ornate brick and terracotta Victorian architecture, using carefully chosen, matching materials. The floor levels of these units – generally three levels plus basement – all differed from the five floors plus basement of Empire House, and those to the Briggate units had to be replaced, in part to accommodate the display windows and to maximise the retail space.

The scheme grew, eventually realising some 4,200 m^2 of sales area, spread over five floors and devoted to fashion wear, accessories, home furnishings and food. The plant and boiler rooms were located at roof level, and staff and storage facilities in the 1,100 m^2 basement, where excavation had to take place in order to provide accommodation for the sprinkler tank.

The existing steel-framed structure of the 1960s building required modification and strengthening in part, with the original atrium to the shopping arcade being infilled, leaving only the smaller escalator-atrium passing full-height through the store. With the increase in sales-floor area came the attendant problem of threading the services through the restricted ceiling voids. To achieve the ventilation requirements, large oval ducts rise up through the sales floors and are clad in vibrant colours.

In addition to the sales areas, the new store also provides a ground-floor espresso bar, with external seating spilling out into Queen Victoria Street under its modern glazed roof, and a 300 m^2 brasserie-style restaurant on the fourth floor with an external Yorkstone terrace overlooking the city.

The design team, in conjunction with project managers Richard Ellis, formulated the client's comprehensive design brief, to be used in their future development programme, and took the scheme forward to planning

MICHAEL PALFREMAN

MICHAEL PALFREMAN

submission. Following tender, with the appointment of
Wimpey Construction UK Limited (Leeds) as Design
and Build contractors, the team were novated to the
contractor to develop the design. At this stage EC
Harris, already acting as the client's quantity surveyors,
were appointed as post-contract project managers.
Shortly after commencement on site in November
1995, Wimpey Construction UK underwent a company
transformation resulting in Tarmac Building taking over
responsibility for the remainder of the construction.
Completed in October 1996, the store opened for trade
in November of that year.

Project Sign-off

After more than ten years of use, the Leeds Harvey
Nichols store has more than delivered on its original
expectations. It has replaced an aged and unsightly
concrete-framed office block, which blighted the vibrant
19th-century architecture of the Victoria Quarter, with
a sleek unassuming 'retail destination'. By the use of
the planar glass frontage, plugging a hole in the street
elevation, the façade is returned to the streetscape and,
conversely, allows the street to flow into the store. The
designers feel that the scheme is a good example of
how to rejuvenate a key element in an existing urban
environment by bringing both new and existing elements
together to honour the past while moving into the future.

The project team believe that this scheme was a key
example for the development and regeneration of Leeds,
and they hope that its success continues to influence
future developments in the city.

MARTINE HAMILTON KNIGHT/BUILT VISION

MICHAEL PALFREMAN

185

There was an extremely tight time schedule in which to gain approval of the brief and to design and detail such a large and complex project on a restricted city-centre site.

LEEDS MAGISTRATES' COURTS

LEEDS DESIGN CONSULTANCY, LEEDS CITY COUNCIL

PO Box 97, Leeds

Construction Value: £21 million
Completion Date: April 1993

Description

A new-build project consisting of 21 courtrooms and ancillary areas, administrative offices, a bridewell and a four-storey car park.

History

The Magistrates' Courts project is a positive contribution to the urban fabric of Leeds, and reinforces the street edge rather than being set back. The building has the strength and clarity of form of its Victorian and Edwardian neighbours, which comprise the character of much of Leeds city centre.

Client's Brief

The brief was for an institution containing 21 courts (12 adult and 9 youth and family courts), a bridewell and all supportive administrative areas. The chosen site was an irregular parcel of land in a prominent location at the western gateway to the city centre.

Design Process

There was an extremely tight time schedule in which to gain approval of the brief and to design and detail such a large and complex project on a restricted city-centre site. The key to its success was the smooth teamwork between the Magistrates' Courts committee members, senior management and the in-house design team of the then Leeds Design Consultancy (now the Strategic Design Alliance) at the city council. A major design challenge in any court building is the requirement to separate the custodial and public circulation routes from those of the magistrates and staff, without compromising the emergency means of escape for each of these groups.

In approaching the design of the building, the basic circulation needed to be clear so as to minimise the amount of directional signing necessary, both on approaching the building and within. This is particularly important in the public areas where visitors, many of whom may well be nervous, should be able to find their way around without being dependent on asking staff or locating and interpreting complex signage.

The largest part of the building, the block of courtrooms, was positioned on the major road frontage of Westgate, with the lower (and subservient) administrative block following the line of Park Street. The bridewell, consisting of 50 cells, was positioned between these two wings. However, the two streets – and consequently the two blocks – are not perpendicular to each other. To resolve this, the pair of blocks are brought together around a circular rooflit space termed the 'Rotunda' – part of the original façade of the Leeds Courthouse, built in 1812 – which extends through the full height of the building and acts as a hinge between the two wings. The major public entrance is located at this prominent corner of the site, where it can clearly be seen as the visitor approaches down Westgate. The entrance lobby leads directly through the Rotunda to the central public lobbies on three levels. These are stacked vertically, with lightwells bringing daylight into the heart of the building.

Magistrates circulate horizontally at the highest level, their corridor providing solar shading to the deep-set windows that light the two upper levels of courtrooms. Secure circulation for defendants and police is provided in another corridor. Vertical circulation for the magistrates is via lifts and stairwells, each of which gives access to a pair of courtrooms – a device which increases the strength and three-dimensionality of the design. The administrative accommodation is located in the wing following the line of Park Street, and the multi-storey car park closes this wing.

Local holding areas are provided so that prisoners are held close to courtrooms in order to speed up

LEEDS MAGISTRATES COURT

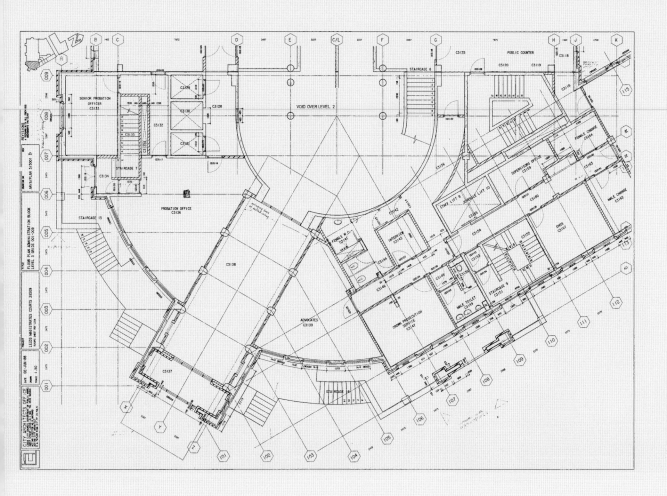

proceedings. Seventeen of the 21 courtrooms are naturally lit, with double floor heights (6 m) and double-storey windows over the custodial circulation areas.

Each of the courtrooms is different in appearance, with various hardwoods for the furniture and doors. A Leeds owl (symbol of the city) is carved into the furniture somewhere in each courtroom.

Project Sign-off

Throughout the initial design briefings and the execution, the architects took into account the building's location in a Conservation Area close to major listed buildings. Materials were used to minimise future maintenance, keeping the overall design in line with the Victorian civic buildings of the city. At the time of construction, it was the largest purpose-built magistrates' court in the UK.

PROJECT TEAM

Client/Building Owner: **Leeds Magistrates' Courts**
Architect: **Leeds Design Consultancy, Leeds City Council**
Quantity Surveyor: **Pritchard Williams & Hunt**

03
SHAPING THE FUTURE

Faster, higher, busier – Leeds must face economic ups and downs like everywhere else, but the city draws on a robust tradition of varied commerce, inventive new ways of making a living and a lively optimism. The energy is guided discreetly by careful thinking and planning which is always up for debate. The future is always and by definition uncertain, but you will seldom meet fewer gloom-mongers than in Yorkshire's de facto capital city.

∧ Cranes have symbolised
Leeds' growth for the
past 25 years
WWW.JH-JPHOTO.CO.UK

'Citizen journalism' is all the rage these days: ordinary people using mobile phones to capture an event or make a brief, digital film of rapid change – wobbly but with an immediacy which gives the right sense of surprise and pace. It is a technique suitable for trying to keep up with the development of Leeds in the first decade of the 21st century. As never before in the city, building is going on everywhere. The pace has inevitably slowed with the financial downturn of 2008 but a familiar streetscape seems to alter almost overnight.

The speed of change may be summarised in two startling figures. In mid-2007, no fewer than 23 separate proposals for buildings of between 20 and 50 storeys, averaging 35, were in the planning system; some are likely to remain fanciful ideas but there are others whose foundations are now actually being laid. The glass shard of Ian Simpson's Lumiere in Wellington Street, commissioned by Kevin Linfoot as the tallest residential development in western Europe at 57 storeys, cost more than £1 million just in planning application processes, geological surveys and similar preliminaries. During the same period, there were potential schemes for a total of 20 bridges across the River Aire. Completion of Lumiere is currently on hold because of the national fall in the property market and the credit squeeze, but the overall momentum is extraordinary; its context is a city whose

palpable buzz and youthful zest are nationally known and repeatedly featured in the media and surveys of the country's most popular and successful communities.

This renaissance is neither shallow nor a bubble; it has deep roots. Plans worth £7.2 billion are in the pipeline, bringing an extra 1.8 million m^2 of office space and hundreds more new flats. Annual output in the city's financial sector topped £13.5 billion in 2006 while the city's traditional strength of 'making things' is buoyant and, as ever in the past, very diverse. Aircraft engines and buses, heart valves and hip joints, foods, cosmetics and all-but-invisible components for IT make Leeds the third-largest manufacturing centre in the UK, with 6 per cent growth in the last decade and 13 per cent forecast for the next. There is no shortage of people wanting to move in to live, work and spend.

What does this mean for the shape of the future? Is the Leeds economy and development market so strong that a free-for-all is under way, or is some hand guiding the unprecedented physical changes in the landscape? If so, what plan is being followed and what will the city look like in 2020? It will unquestionably have altered more dramatically than at any other time in its long history. The transformation between 1990 and 2008, let alone what is to come next, has left the massive rebuilding of Victorian Leeds far behind in scale.

∧ Red brick continues as a
trademark Leeds building
material. The 'Leeds Look'
WWW.JH-JPHOTO.CO.UK

There is no single hand on the tiller, but many. No rigid masterplan, but a supple interpretation of the main players' and partners' agreed approach. Partnership has become second nature to Leeds, but the team is different, larger and more varied than the duo that guided the late-20th-century period of major regeneration. There is no longer a Leeds Development Corporation as an alternative centre of power and decisive action, so Leeds City Council bears most responsibility – a more accurate word in contemporary Britain than 'power'. Central governments, both Conservative and Labour, have destroyed the old hegemony of the town halls, but Leeds has not hankered after that for many years. The council is committed to working with the people who have the greatest ability and resources to make things happen: the private-sector businessmen and, increasingly, women who are prepared to risk capital on speculative development.

This friendly and productive way of working is so familiar in Leeds that it can take an outsider to underline how important and effective it is. One such is the architect Graham Morrison, guest assessor at the Leeds Architecture Awards 2006. The kernel of his speech was admiration for the way that developers in the city now 'come to the table with packages that take into account the whole picture and not just their corner of it'. The process had gained national attention, he said, and left him in no doubt whatever that 'anyone with any sense would enjoy the prospect of living here and becoming part of a great future'.

It would be foolish to pretend that the relationship is always a love-fest. Developers can overstep the mark in terms of flinging up buildings too hastily; the much-derided 'Leeds Look' sometimes seems to be in danger of having an early-21st-century successor – buildings uniformly hung with terracotta and grey rainscreen cladding. Democracy and the planning process can sometimes frustrate the loans, networks and careful timing which make a new building possible. But the principle of partnership is not at issue, and Leeds has a structure that ensures that it happens at every level. The council's statutory system of cross-party executive boards and scrutiny is mirrored on the private-sector side by joint organisations in which potential rivals

make common ground. Principal among them on the development front are the Chamber of Commerce and its Leeds Property Forum, while the Leeds Initiative continues to bring public and private together in a series of powerful specialist groups.

The latest, Renaissance Leeds, involves a newer and bigger partner: Yorkshire Forward, the regional development agency (RDA) for Yorkshire and the Humber, which has a generous budget and the muscle that comes from government goodwill. Labour and Liberal Democrat dreams of an elected regional assembly collapsed through public lack of interest in 2004, but the RDAs were not affected by that. Their role has always been an economic rather than a political one: that of powerful enabling bodies getting on with a practical job – in many ways an expansion of the role of the government's regional offices, of which most people in the street have never heard. The greater part of Yorkshire Forward's work involves regeneration, which takes it outside Leeds to the less successful parts of the region. But it has shown a particular and strikingly imaginative interest in architecture and design, and this has brought it into the city's existing partnerships with the third phase of its Renaissance Programme.

This is the operation which drew national headlines when the 'starchitect' Will Alsop drew up plans to turn Barnsley into a Yorkshire version of an Italian hill village in 2001, complete with a halo created by searchlights mounted on the Town Hall. This was primarily intended as a spur to local thinking, although some actual demolition and rebuilding has since gone on. Meanwhile the notion of renaissance and its crucial complement of additional government funding has been rolled out across the region, and Renaissance Leeds has seen a group of other leading lights from the contemporary architectural world turn their attention to Leeds. As in the partnership between the council and developers, there are forums where the city and these regional players meet. The government's enthusiasm for 'city-regions' after the elected assembly debacle has brought the two concepts together in the same way as the hyphenated words, and the resulting Northern Way Initiative is based on successful cities such as Leeds thinking and working in a regional context rather than alone.

∧ Kirkstall valley
WWW.JH-JPHOTO.CO.UK

So those are the main players. These are their aims: much the favourite phrase in discussions of Leeds' future is 'going up a league', for all the misfortunes which have attended Leeds United Football Club. With due respect to Sheffield, Bradford and Hull, the city has established itself as the regional capital. The next step is European status. You can enjoy a game collecting the different role models cited in debates about this, from Barcelona to Valencia via Milan. Whichever is preferred by the different participants in discussions, it is cities of that calibre which Leeds intends to match, and, this being Yorkshire, overtake. To do so, it needs an interesting combination. Gilda Porcelli singing Italian opera to her customers at her Pasta Romagna café in Albion Place is part of it. More drily, so are the rocketing statistics of employment in the local financial services sector. Membership of the European City club requires economic prosperity, allure for tourists, some institutions of European significance (they may be cultural, sporting, financial or political) and, of course, classy architecture and planning, new as well as old.

The future shape of Leeds is therefore at the top of the agenda for going up a league, and there are plentiful

'road maps' which set out the route between today and the commonly accepted target of 2020. An important one is the compulsory Unitary Development Plan and its successor, the more consultative structure of the Local Development Framework which is currently in draft form, with their foundation of establishing land uses. From this basis, more detailed agreements deal with the future of the city centre, the inner and outer suburbs and the final ring of countryside, market towns and the thin but precious green borders with Wakefield, Kirklees and Bradford. Indeed Leeds and Bradford are working closely together on a range of issues, especially linkages in transport, housing and the economy which together have been given the title of the 'Leeds–Bradford Corridor Project'. A fundamental part of the Vision for Leeds is Narrowing the Gap, a programme of measures designed to help less affluent areas catch up with their more prosperous neighbours. All the time, the property market is bubbling with suppressed energy as it presses for progress on the few but obvious gaps which remain in the cityscape after the 1960s–90s regeneration.

These gaps are being filled almost by the month. Most notably, the last of the large, sensitive but undeveloped

<< Bill Bremner's
statue greets Leeds
United fans at
Elland Road
WWW.JH-JPHOTO.CO.UK

< Gilda Porcelli
(Pasta Romagna)
WWW.JH-JPHOTO.CO.UK

194

^ The Rose Bowl site
WWW.JH-JPHOTO.CO.UK

and tatty holes right in the city centre have been sorted out after lengthy debate about prospective new-build's purpose, density and look. All through the increasingly prosperous years, right at the heart of the boom and 'zing', two big empty quarters were used as temporary car parks on either side of the Lower Headrow – one of them forming a large hole in Lady Lane and the former Leylands (in the middle of Leeds' embryonic Chinatown), the other stretching up to the faux-Oriental glories of bustling Kirkgate Market. Equally crucial to the future shape of Leeds, another temporary car park with a famously peculiar surface of shredded rubber particles occupied a prime site behind the Civic Hall, an area enlarged by the demolition of the Hall's unlovely office extension.

John Lewis and other major stores are now booked into the old Chinatown space, with a magnificent extension of the Grand Arcade planned to run down the hill from Vicar Lane. New-build will combine with restoration of fine but long-forlorn parts of the city centre's heritage, such as the former Central Methodist Mission in Lady Lane – a building interestingly constructed with stonework from a Roman Catholic church which it replaced. At the time of writing, concrete, glass and

steel are already rising in the space behind the Civic Hall for the £45 million Portland Gate scheme of academic faculties and restaurants for Leeds Metropolitan University. The scheme, designed by Sheppard Robson, is known as The Rose Bowl. It carries the hopes of Simon Lee, the energetic vice chancellor of Leeds Met, for an iconic building to match the university's other high-profile initiatives such as the partnership with Yorkshire county cricket club which has led to the venerable Test and rugby league ground in Leeds being renamed Headingley Carnegie, after Leeds Met's Carnegie sports departments. The Rose Bowl in this instance is a glass sphere standing approximately 20 m tall on legs as the focal point of a building which is otherwise designed to relate to the neighbouring Civic Hall, a signature work of 20th-century Leeds designed by Vincent Harris and completed in 1933. The bowl itself contains lecture theatres, while the rest of the building combines classrooms with more informal places such as coffee bars to mix and exchange ideas.

This project has particular interest as an architectural testing ground for two other powerful members of the Leeds partnership: Leeds University and Leeds Metropolitan University can already claim European

195

^ Student flats mushroom
  opposite Leeds University
  WWW.JH-JPHOTO.CO.UK

^ Student street life in Headingley
  WWW.JH-JPHOTO.CO.UK

status, and both have plans – and the means – for an expansion which, city council officers say after initial discussions with the academics, could involve 'staggering sums'. One of their emerging skyscrapers, by Feilden Clegg Bradley Studios, is on the former BBC site at the bottom of Blenheim Terrace in Woodhouse Lane. Up at the top of the terrace, eye-catching curved flats for students have changed the skyline opposite the main frontage of Leeds University. A 25-year growth in student numbers in Leeds to over 115,000 (compared with the city's total workforce of 457,400) has already had other dramatic effects. A youthful triangle has its apex in Woodhouse Lane and its base at the far end of Headingley – a suburb so perfectly suited to students that a study by Leeds Metropolitan University calls it a 'Shangri-La' for young people, to which they will return in their dreams for their rest of their life, like the heroine of Daphne du Maurier's *Rebecca*. Not everyone in the neighbourhood sees it like that; attempts continue to limit student occupation and safeguard primary schools and other essentials of family life. But both the student quarter and the effect of so many young people on the food, drink, entertainment and night-time economy of Leeds are essential to any Munich/Amsterdam ambitions.

Consultation over all these sites has been thorough, and the design solutions have been guided by the City Centre Urban Design Strategy of 2002 which Councillor Liz Minkin characterised as 'making places work for people'. Its road map followed four themes – form, movement, space and use – so that, in Liz's words, 'using the established character of the city centre as a starting point developers, designers and architects can produce original buildings which reinforce and develop the individuality of Leeds.' These four themes merit closer attention:

The Form section of the road map calls for attention to detail rather than grandiose planning. Special attention should be paid to street corners; activity should be encouraged by siting the main entrances of buildings on busy streets, parks or squares; new façades should be made from diverse materials, which also contrast with existing buildings where appropriate; 'gateway' buildings should mark the main entrances to the centre, in a larger version of the structures created in the 1980s for the pedestrian precinct by Landmark Leeds.

The Movement theme demands obvious features such as easier pedestrian links and better-organised car parking, but, more originally, also emphasises the importance of 'sequential views for people entering and using the city by train, bus, car, bicycle, boat or on foot'. Although this is easier said than done, the principle is nonetheless established that Leeds must become simpler and more enjoyable to navigate. You only have to visit any outlying part of Yorkshire and ask locals how they find their way around when they go shopping in Leeds, to understand just how necessary improvements in this aspect of the city are. As a result, a major city-centre signage and 'legibility' study is currently in

v The canal provides
  a serene green
  pathway to the
  city's heart
  WWW.JH-JPHOTO.CO.UK

progress. As for simple enjoyment of the cityscape, the inclusion of boats among the means of transport is significant. Along with arriving rail passengers, anyone who has sailed a canal barge or walked the towpath west of the station knows the beautiful bend of the river Aire and the Leeds–Liverpool Canal, side by side, through a curve of tousled greenery backed by two mature weeping willows, whose beauty is worthy of a Chinese willow-pattern dinner plate. The fact that these trees were spared by Gordon Carey's 2003 building on Whitehall Road is hugely significant. It preserved a tranquil haven which dates back to Sandy Lobby, the shallow beach where Leeds people picnicked and swam before the Industrial Revolution.

The Space theme deserves particular attention, as one of the issues which has risen most rapidly to the top of the 'from here to 2020' agenda. Leeds has some claim historically to be an unusually green city, thanks partly to far-sighted council purchases such as Roundhay Park (bitterly controversial at the time) and donations from wealthy citizens, notably Colonel Thomas North's gift of Kirkstall Abbey. But the city does not have the

striking, tree-lined approach boulevards of Birmingham and the density of early-21st-century development has caused concern. Strikingly, this has come from private developers as well as the public; in the autumn of 2005 Kevin Linfoot of K W Linfoot published a report commissioned from Leeds University's geography department which was a cry for more green. 'The strength of feeling about lack of green space and lack of facilities really surprised us,' said Rachael Unsworth who wrote the report, 'there needs to be a strategic approach about incorporating green space in the local development framework. Natural elements really seem to matter to people and evidence of that is seen in prices. Apartments by the water command a 20 per cent premium.' This strategic approach is set out through the Space theme and the city has subsequently developed tactical policies, such as a requirement for a generous proportion of open space in all new developments, in order to put the strategy into action.

The Space theme also identifies opportunities for shaping a special look for Leeds through bespoke railings – the Victorian examples in the Civic Quarter

197

∧ Kenneth Armitage RA's
16 ft sculpture *Both Arms*
in Millennium Square
WWW.JH-JPHOTO.CO.UK

∧ The city's symbolic owls
guard the Town Hall
WWW.JH-JPHOTO.CO.UK

∨ The Carriageworks Theatre
in Millennium Square and
Chelsea Flower Show Garden
WWW.JH-JPHOTO.CO.UK

which use the city's owl symbol are splendid exemplars of how well this can be done. More public art and distinctive street furniture are part of the same 'crusade'. Miniparks have a vigorous promoter in Councillor Andrew Carter, leader of the Conservative group and alternate leader of the council with his Liberal Democrat coalition partner – first Mark Harris, and, since 2007, Richard Brett – each party taking the leadership for six months at a time. Carter was instrumental in the resiting of Leeds' award-winning garden from the 2004 Chelsea Flower Show to Roundhay Park. He is now working on bringing back its successor, which won the show's silver medal in 2007 with the Scent of a Roman Garden, and may find a place for it between the universities and the city centre. This year's garden (2008) called The Largest Room in the House won silver gilt and is due to be installed in Roundhay Park.

Finally, the Use theme places a great emphasis on bustle and activity. If people are to be encouraged to live in Leeds as well as work there, the city must be moulded to encourage street life – sauntering, sitting, playing with children, listening to music as well as the evening and late-night drinking which sometimes seems to pass for the '24-hour city' of tourism promoters' dreams.

∧ The old Central Station
site with its former truck-
lifting tower
WWW.JH-JPHOTO.CO.UK

∧ Sir Leonard Hutton
gates at Headingley Test
cricket ground
WWW.JH-JPHOTO.CO.UK

Two developments on the banks of the river Aire are about to be useful testbeds for this approach. The first is Wellington Place, the new name for the former muddle of retail, warehouse and parking surrounding a fascinating old lifting tower that survives from the Great Northern and other railway companies' station and goods yard which previously occupied the site. Both the tower and the fine Victorian bridge across the Aire will be restored as part of MEPC's mixed development of homes, offices, leisure outlets and shops but the most intriguing Use element will be a beach. This might be eyebrow-raising in a Northern British city, but it draws on the pre-industrial tradition of local people swimming and picnicking on the Aire's gentle curve here, at the very site of Sandy Lobby. Its revival is in the hands of the American landscape architect Martha Schwartz's practice while the development architects are Fielden Clegg Bradley Studios working with the local practice careyjones.

Closer to the station, the enthusiastic Leeds developer Len Davies spent a couple of decades from 1980 trying to extend his 'retail festival' shops in the atmospheric Dark Arches beneath the platforms on to the adjacent cleared area beside the Leeds–Liverpool canal's terminus basin. Success finally eluded him – and perhaps the car parking on the site was too lucrative – and his interest was acquired by Isis who are currently on site. Their scheme consists of three very different buildings that are nonetheless intended to read as a family. Two are residential blocks and the third a hotel and all will have bars and cafés on the ground floor. Following the Use theme, these hope to bring life to new public space beside the dock, south facing and waterside with the added interest of barges, wildfowl and maybe bathers drying off after a spell at the beach. Isis' trio of architects are careyjones, who have designed a 20-storey cylindrical tower, Allies and Morrison for the scheme's L-shaped hotel and CZWG for the wedge-shaped residential building which completes this

'family'. There are plenty of sceptics who are worried about its sheer size. Time will tell.

The City Centre Urban Design Strategy meanwhile rests on a series of more local briefs: for example, the Leeds Waterfront Strategy uses a similarly themed structure to highlight Uses (promote a diversity of land and water based uses), Links (provide a network of pedestrian and cycle routes), Character (establish a landscape character framework) and Development (designate a series of destination nodes with distinctive character). Other focused studies are being organised for the suburbs and the rural fringe through Neighbourhood Design Statements – often initiated by local community groups but ultimately forming planning guidance for defining, protecting and promoting the character of the varying pieces of the Leeds 'jigsaw'. A good example covers northern Headingley, where one of the first Statements was organised in 2005 by the Far Headingley Village Society, an amenity group full of articulate professionals. Its success encouraged them to ally with equally savvy groups in central and southern Headingley to ask for an Area Action Plan, a further tier of design guidance which the city council can initiate if enough local people ask them to do so.

To complete this intensive scrutiny of just one area, a £10, 50-page, full-colour booklet called 'Headingley Renaissance' was published in November 2005, providing a 'vision to guide the future development of Central Headingley in accordance with the aspirations and priorities identified by the local community, and following sustainable community principles'. An action plan agreed with the council's Inner North West Area Committee is now being implemented. Headingley is admittedly one of the best-known suburbs of Leeds, with a genuinely international icon in the shape of its test cricket and rugby league ground. But its people have certainly made clear in this raft of planning guidance, and hundreds of specific proposals and

199

targets, what they feel the shape of their part of the city should be, with controversially dense redevelopment plans for the former Leeds Girls High School site currently keeping discussions on the boil.

A cynic might suggest that no amount of planning will do as much to bring satisfactory public gain about as simple economic muscle: if Leeds continues to boom, its growing city-centre population will insist on having parks, corner shops and schools as they settle down and their children grow. Hard-headed as this assessment might be, there is every reason for optimism here; it is not a bubble of speculation which is driving the astonishing rate of central apartment building – over 3,500 flats in the centre, nearly another 3,000 being built, 4,400 more with planning permission and an estimated 7,000 on top of that in various stages of the planning system. The force behind this is the growth in financial and business services and related modern sectors, such as Internet companies and telephone-based services (a much wider category than the simple 'call-centre' handling orders or customer complaints). Financial and related service jobs have risen from 27,500 in 1981 to 45,000 in 1991 to over 114,000 in 2007, and account for most of the extra 48,000 jobs which the city expects to have attracted by 2011. The enormous flow of Internet traffic through the city, which is the birthplace of Freeserve and Planet Online, is also certain to increase.

Talk of success and boom, however, always triggers a reaction in Leeds – usually a valid one. What about the downside: the inner-city areas and peripheral estates which still have some of the worst deprivation statistics in Britain? A council report on providing affordable housing, 'Making the Housing Ladder Work', warned in 2007 that only four of Leeds' 102 postcode sectors (3.9 per cent of the whole) had housing affordable to those on below-average single incomes. A second slogan joins 'Going up a league' in this context: 'Narrowing the gap'. In the same way that the merits of partnership have become ingrained in the city's psyche, this side to shaping the future city also has healthy roots. In the 1990s, the practically minded council leadership of Brian Walker, Jon Trickett's Labour successor, repeatedly raised concern that Leeds was becoming a 'two-speed city'. The pizzazz of Harvey Nichols and the 24-hour clubs obscured alarming levels of poverty and unemployment in nearby wards. Walker was a long-term thinker with an engaging lack of interest in who eventually got the credit for successful change. One of his quiet achievements was the rescue of Oulton Hall, one of a number of fine stately homes south of Leeds, which fell into such disrepair that by the 1970s it was little more than a fire-blackened stone shell. This is hard to believe for anyone now enjoying the luxury hotel in the restored mansion, or the golf course which Walker secured as part of a multi-million-pound private/public-sector deal.

v New flats and
apartments
near market
WWW.JH-JPHOTO.CO.UK

ⱯⱯⱯ Otley from the Chevin
WWW.JH-JPHOTO.CO.UK

ⱯⱯ A modern prospect of 'Green Leeds'
WWW.JH-JPHOTO.CO.UK

Ʌ Out for a walk in the unbroken
green belt, Allerton Bywater
WWW.JH-JPHOTO.CO.UK

The calculations behind these fears about 'two-speed Leeds' can sometimes be a little simplistic. The government's index of local deprivation is a blunt instrument which fails to record the distinctive vigour and local character of such places as Chapeltown and Harehills, which have in the past hit the headlines for the wrong reasons. But a good, overall point was being made, and, typically of Walker, it was also a practical one when it came to bidding for deprivation money from the European Union and Whitehall. Taken as a whole, Leeds was a successful city which also made much of its success in marketing terms. This might seem to disqualify any hope of deprivation funding, but the two-speed analysis made a convincing and accurate case that parts of the whole were not sharing in the general prosperity and genuinely ranked with the likes of Halifax and Wakefield. In a far-reaching triumph for Walker and his team, Leeds won a handsome share of £216 million given to Yorkshire by the EU in 2001 to help hoist

up deprived areas, along with £63.4 million over nine years to 2008 from the government's Neighbourhood Renewal Fund, which had similar objectives to the EU's programme. Labour's successors in the Liberal Democrat, Conservative and Green alliance followed in the same tradition in 2006 by winning £15 million over three years through the government's Local Enterprise Growth Initiative.

Leeds continues to build on this, with a strategy for the next 12 years to 2020, through a series of programmes and consultations similar to those which have been so well supported in Headingley. The process was given a spur by the creation of 16 Community Involvement Teams in all areas of the city – bodies made up of all the elected members in each of the 16 areas, which bring together appointed and invited local people rather than directly elected ones. From the purely democratic point of view, the statutory parish councils requested and won by local people in Horsforth, Otley, Allerton

201

∧∧∧ Near Kippax
WWW.JH-JPHOTO.CO.UK

∧∧ Thorner
WWW.JH-JPHOTO.CO.UK

∧ Pudsey
WWW.JH-JPHOTO.CO.UK

Bywater and other suburbs are in another league. But the CITs – and their successors the ten Area Committees, which took over in 2004 – have generally been neither exclusive nor excluding, and it has not been hard for opinionated or active local people to contribute and influence matters. The committees have increasingly robust functions, more money, extra powers and improved service delivery in fields such as youth affairs. Local forums, effectively mini-Leeds Initiatives, underpin the basic structure of five inner-city and five outer Area Committees.

The second Vision for Leeds report, produced by the public/private-sector partners at the Leeds Initiative in 2004, also placed much of its emphasis on the need to narrow dramatically the difference between the city's dual speeds before 2020. It was in the local arena for two years and the Liberal Democrat ex-council leader Mark Harris – a shrewd and witty man with a distinctive, gravelly voice box after successfully fighting throat cancer – had good grounds for claiming at the launch in July 2004 that 'this is a document that everyone can unite behind.' It was superficially easy for that to happen because Vision 2 explicitly tackled the issue of outer areas risking falling behind the core, rather like a set of gears in which the outer rings spin much less rapidly than the central ones. Harris remarked: 'Of course the city centre is vital to the success of Leeds and its wider region. But the Vision strongly recognises that Leeds is a place of many parts and there are important priorities in the inner city, the market towns, rural areas and the district centres as well.'

At the time, Harris had only been council leader for three weeks and he acknowledged that credit for driving forward Vision 2 should go to the previous Labour administration led by Brian Walker, and latterly Keith Wakefield after Walker lost his Rothwell seat to the Liberal Democrats. But Harris was able to give the talk of common purpose some personal muscle by summarising his unusually mixed biography as a private-sector businessman from an ethnic (Jewish) minority who has also been left, by his cancer, with a Grade 1 disability. As he said at the launch, his personal charcteristics encapsulated the sense of inclusion that so much of Vision 2 was about.

His successor as head of the Lib Dems, Richard Brett, alternates his leadership with the leader of the Conservative group, Councillor Andrew Carter, who started his working life as a trainee with the architects Harry Webster and Partners in Leeds' Blenheim Terrace. He changed course after a few years and went on to a successful career in textiles, but an interest in design and urban planning has stayed with him. As the council's executive member for development and regeneration, he has been the political leader most closely involved in shaping Leeds since the alliance took over from Labour. He emphasises the importance of a 'fine balancing act' between the pace of new building and the city's impressive existing architectural heritage – a challenge which he faces with optimism after visiting Boston in the United States. 'There they have a lot of historic areas but the city has been able to take new and sometimes very tall buildings because they got

^ Looking westwards over developing
Armley to the Pennine moors
WWW.JH-JPHOTO.CO.UK

the design and siting right,' he says. 'That's the challenge
we face – to get new building to complement the existing
city. I've watched Leeds develop in my lifetime with
enormous pride, and I know we can do it. The only time
the city nearly dropped a clanger was when everyone
went overboard for the "Leeds Look", but common
sense prevailed and we pulled back from that in time.
Leeds has been lucky to have had a tradition of steady
progress, regardless of which party has been in charge.'

The change of political control in 2004, after 24
years of the same party in power, nonetheless had
some direct effects. For one, it brought the interests
of the rural wards higher up the city's agenda. Out
of 99 city councillors representing 33 wards, a third
are from areas which cannot really be classed as
'urban', although that does not always mean that they
are geographically far from the centre. In a recent
exchange at the council's development headquarters in
the Leonardo Building, the Civic Architect John Thorp
celebrated the fact that he could stand at the top of
Albion Street and see someone ploughing on the hillside
beyond Holbeck and Hunslet known as 'back of Ida's'.
Peter Vaughan countered that he enjoyed being able to
see lambs in the fields beside Temple Newsam from a
similar, central viewpoint.

To encourage outreach from the centre, the city has sent
ambassadors for good design into areas such as Armley,
dominated by the great black castle of Leeds prison, and
Wortley, out of sight of the centre behind the western
hills and so consequently often 'out of mind'. This is
where you will find the buzzy figure of Jonathan Morgan,
one of the key developers in the early days of Leeds'
cool city-centre loft apartments. He now sits on the West
Leeds Gateway Regeneration Board: a public/private
partnership with a sense of urgency – and which, in that
sense, is a local equivalent of the Leeds Initiative – with
a duty to galvanise 'second speed' suburbs. The board
is charged with spreading the 'city centre spirit' to these
outlying red-brick terraces, and has duly begun to do
so. The unlikely setting of land opposite Mike's Carpets

premises at Mistress Lane has been chosen for a design
competition on the theme of 'Gateway to Armley'. The
eyesore of the old Liberal Club is to be demolished (no
sentiment there from Leeds' new political co-masters)
as a start to sprucing up the attractive but dowdy
buildings of Armley Town Street, and the depressing
state of The Clydes Estate is to receive the attention of
bright-minded designers.

Crucial to this approach is a recognition of Armley's and
Wortley's existing virtues at the Leeds end of the Leeds–
Bradford Corridor. This exercise is not the arrival of
narrow-minded missionaries in a backward land. Morgan
is very canny and knows that student housing demand
has already spilt across the valley to Armley from
increasingly high-priced Headingley, Burley and Hyde
Park. He and his colleagues were not at all surprised,
either, to find that many families on The Clydes who
deplore the rundown state of their neighbourhood
nonetheless love its position. Their houses are just a
walk from Leeds centre past the celebrated Armley
Gyratory roundabout – the latter, part of the city's
folklore owing to its virtually daily starring role in local-
radio traffic-jam bulletins (along with that other icon of
Leeds' rush-hour snarl-up, the Ingram Road Distributor).
Armley is also close to the runaway success story of
Holbeck Urban Village, where the rundown old industrial
heartland of Leeds is being revived as a centre of high-
tech economic muscle.

The same approach is under way in Farnley and Wortley
ward further out from the centre, assisted by the Green
Party, initially part of the council's ruling coalition,
whose local energy has made the ward their Leeds
power base. Here, too, there are many local assets to
be realised, from leafy streets to historical links such
as the birthplace of Phil May. A rakish, floppy-fringed
figure with a perpetual cigar, he was a colossus of Leeds'
sometimes forgotten period as a national focus of cool,
arty style at the end of the 19th century – an Aubrey
Beardsley 'without the smut'. Moving round the compass,
similar exercises are beginning to regenerate East Leeds,

203

∧ Sovereign Street: one of the last major
development sites in central Leeds
WWW.JH-JPHOTO.CO.UK

the lower Aire Valley, Beeston and Little London.

The links between these areas are high in the planners'
and developers' minds too. Vision 2 sees the whole
as well as the parts, and transport is essential to this
process. There has been interminable discussion on this
topic, in Leeds just as nationally, but trying to anchor
strategies to the reality of new roads, cycleways and
public transport appears to be the devil's own job. Any
such plans need a long run-in for laying-out, property-
buying and obtaining planning permission and funds; but
this process additionally has to contend with constantly
changing policies at national level, as the great debate
over car use swings to and fro. Leeds is at the forefront
of imaginative experiments: the 'two plus' lane reserved
for car-sharers in rush hours up Stanningley Lane is
a much-cited national model. So, too, is the guided
bus system along Scott Hall Road. But the city is all
too conscious that the people who make the very big
funding decisions in this field are elsewhere.

The long but frustratingly vain struggle for Supertram
is the most obvious example of this dilemma. The
proposed network would have given an enormous hand
to Leeds' going up a league. Its very name makes the
point, even if teased by the likes of the Leeds Guide
which entertainingly fantasised: 'You mean a tram
that can fly and see through buildings?' But central
government withheld approval for funding even after
very large sums had been spent on preparations,
including some compulsory purchase of property on
the proposed routes. They decided, slowly in Leeds'
view which was subsequently upheld by a critical report
from the National Audit Office, that most previous
tram schemes had not lived up to budget, passenger
and road-traffic-reduction hopes. The best hope is for
consolation-prize money for the new priority – making
better use of trains and high-tech buses.

This has been an uncharacteristic setback to the sense

of progress which is now carrying Leeds towards 2020.
The spirit of the city is better shown in the scale and
quality of the new developments described in this book.
Once the 'holes' beside the Lower Headrow and behind
the Civic Hall are filled, there is a general consensus
that the northern bank of the River Aire will be, as one
planner puts it, 'full up'. As a result, Leeds' centre
of gravity is moving south. The old London Midland
Railway viaduct offers a potential green path or cycleway
through the mix of restored heritage buildings and new
developments in Holbeck Urban Village and the Round
Foundry, a combination of old and new which does
justice to the memory of Leeds' engineering hero of
the Industrial Revolution, Matthew Murray. In this same
area, the tower of Bridgewater Place hoists the city
skyline to an entirely new level: a 30-storey pillar which
would have delighted another local lad, John Smeaton,
who built the 'unbuildable' lighthouse on Eddystone
Rock. Briefly the tallest building in the North of England,
Bridgewater has already confidently stood in for London
skyscrapers in a number of TV dramas (it's cheaper and
friendlier to film in Leeds). It will be the southernmost
of a spine of high towers that is going to be the most
dramatic change in the shape of Leeds. Several of
them, such as Ian Simpson's planned 'Kissing Towers'
on Swinegate, have the potential to fill that long-empty
space in the city centre marked 'Reserved for Icon'.
When the market recovers, the same architect's 54-
and 32-storey Lumiere, next to Linfoot's conversion of
the former Post Office in Wellington Street, will surely
challenge it for that title.

Other towers, which will give the Leeds horizon the look
of a US-style 'downtown' with a trademark cluster of
skyscrapers, are zoned to step down, and reflect the
contours of, the ridge from the Parkinson Building's
tower at Leeds University to Jan Fletcher's proposed
40-storey mixed-use development in Holbeck. The
novelties of the K2 building, in its day considered

204

awesomely high and unusually stylish on top (it still merits the last description), are being dwarfed by plans for 'sausages', 'spikes' and even a 'poppadam building' by Ken Shuttleworth on the site of the Leeds International Pool. The former regional headquarters of the BBC at Broadcasting House in Woodhouse Lane are earmarked for one of these icons; others may double as gateways to the city centre. The energy involved has an American, pioneering feel to it.

The emphasis, however, is by no means all on height. Leeds is pioneering genuinely 'green' buildings, with schemes which include one of the country's first truly carbon-neutral developments at the former hostel for the homeless, Shaftesbury House. Small-scale windmills are joining traditional street and skyline furniture. Sustainability will be central to ambitious plans put in train by both the universities to develop their neighbouring estates. The skimpiness of some of the initial student housing blocks which have sprung up on the fringe of the campuses has been replaced by the quality shown in, for example, Feilden Clegg Bradley Studio's project on the old BBC site.

Leeds' city council's own architects have also earned praise for sustainability in the new school buildings which sprang up after 2000 as a result of Private Finance Initiative deals. New Bewerley is a notable example, giving the inner-city suburb of Beeston a striking £4.5 million shell-shaped building which combines a new primary, formed from two merged schools, with a children's centre and integrated learning centre. Over on the eastern fringe of Leeds, a much larger-scale exercise in sustainable housing is under way, after initial delays, at the 'Millennium Village' transformation of the former colliery village of Allerton Bywater. Initially, contractors were unable to meet the vision of English Partnerships, but a revised masterplan by the urban designers Edaw has seen the ground broken. Miller Homes are building houses on a 'homezone' pattern not unlike local initiatives which have made 'green' communities out of the Methleys in Chapel Allerton and Littlemoor in Rawdon, and Fusion are building highly sustainable housing alongside.

A further element in the procession of new and potential developments is style. The transformation of the Grand Theatre and former Assembly Rooms into a stunning permanent home for Opera North has shown the way, from the glories of the restored architecture to the marvellous mechanics of its lorry lift. Simply standing and watching an entire truck being hoisted up from street level to the second floor in order to unload scenery, machinery and props is one of Leeds' new entertainments and a sensation in itself. Going further back in history, Kirkstall Abbey and Temple Newsam House, two of the finest buildings in Leeds, have been sensitively repaired and Roundhay Park has undergone a thorough restoration. The retail extravaganza around Eastgate will, meanwhile, be just that: a veritable festival of consumerism. At the time of writing, we are promised roof gardens and a vaulting, glass-topped passaggio which will bring Leeds' great tradition of arcades to a climax – a successor to the neighbouring Victoria Quarter on the scale of the Victor Emmanuel arcade in

∧∧∧ The K2 flats
WWW.JH-JPHOTO.CO.UK

∧∧ Student flats on
Burley Road
WWW.JH-JPHOTO.CO.UK

∧ Millennium Village,
Allerton Bywater
WWW.JH-JPHOTO.CO.UK

^ Headrow Hole
WWW.JH-JPHOTO.CO.UK

^ Holy Trinity, Boar Lane
RICHARD MORAN / WWW.MORANPHOTO.CO.UK

Milan. Outline permission has been given for all these as part of a £700 million plan by Town Centre Securities and Hammerson to fill the big 'Headrow Hole' on either side of Eastgate, which will go under the working title of the Harewood and Eastgate Quarter.

At pedestrian level, measures to improve lighting, waymarking and the overall 'legibility' of the central streetscape are also in hand. Landmark Leeds, the great pioneer in its day and still the core of Leeds' pedestrianised centre, is to be reworked. There will be other new attractions for the signs and lights to point out. Holy Trinity in Boar Lane is set to become a visual and performing arts centre as well as a church, and the Gilbert Scott infirmary building has been sketched and measured for a winter gardens. On the edge of the booming centre, more than a billion pounds of investment has gone into East Street in the last five years; and the long-awaited curve of the inner ring road's Stage Seven, essentially the circle's missing southern link, looks out on stilts to the great Victorian factories of the Aire Valley which are scheduled for transformation in their turn. A third of all the space available for new employment use in West Yorkshire lies here, where the river leaves the city of Leeds and turns south.

Westwards from Granary Wharf, a swathe of properties between the River Aire and Kirkstall Road has meanwhile come on to the market together, offering potential to spread the city centre west as well as south. The bus depot is moving, the dairy has relocated to Stourton and the biggest of them all, the Yorkshire Chemicals works, has relocated out of town. This last is one of the mightiest surviving relics of old 'factoryopolis' Leeds, complete with its own blast zone in case potentially

dangerous processes go wrong. The scale of potential redevelopment is equally huge. To kickstart thinking about it in 2004, the long-established Leeds architect Ian Tod, whose work was influential in the earliest years of riverside renovation at the Calls, drew up a plan of Napoleonic proportions which trailed the notion of a Second City Centre from Westgate to the honey-coloured railway viaduct between Armley and Burley. His deliberatively provocative sketches showed blocks and grids, squares and a tree-lined boulevard between the river and Kirkstall Road – a masterplan, now being worked on by other architects and planners, to show that 'big thinking' does not stop at the boundaries of central Leeds.

In the same way, but on the other side of both the river and the city centre, another vast space is about to open up with the withdrawal of Yorkshire Chemicals' other Leeds plant and its surrounding blast zone. Sensitively placed opposite the Royal Armouries, this represents an obvious development challenge in itself but it could be part of something much bigger. The site leads southwards into Hunslet, home of some of the other remaining titanic buildings from the factory age such as Britannia Mills and the Alf Cooke works. A patchwork of still-flourishing small industries and workshops squashed in between will be under pressure to sell out or succumb to inevitably rising rents and leases as this part of Leeds becomes sought after in its turn. As along the Kirkstall Road from Westgate, strategic thinking will need to be the order of the day.

Impetus for such thinking is coming from the different levels of planning discussion – from Neighbourhood Design Statements to the Local Development Framework

< Yorkshire Chemicals,
Kirkstall Road
WWW.JH-JPHOTO.CO.UK

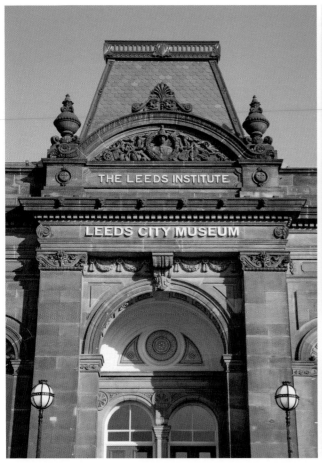

∧ The new museum's entrance
on Millennium Square
WWW.JH-JPHOTO.CO.UK

∧ Auguste Rodin's *Age of Bronze* in the
entrance to the City Art Gallery
WWW.JH-JPHOTO.CO.UK

– but with extra energy from Yorkshire Forward's Renaissance team. The experts chosen to look at Leeds were headed by two US practices, both high profile enough to satisfy the city's international ambitions. The Michael Sorkin Studio, based in New York, has a track record of sustainable urban design in San Francisco and the development of experimental loft housing. Sorkin is also professor of urbanism at the academy of fine arts in Vienna. Koetter Kim, an international urban design and architecture practice based in Boston and London, was responsible for the masterplan at Canary Wharf, the 'new city' in London's former docklands.

They worked with Urban Initiatives of London and Dublin, whose masterplan at King's Cross and St Pancras is familiar to visitors from Leeds arriving at Yorkshire's two rail termini in the capital. Urbed, the Urban and Economic Development Group based in Manchester as well as London, add a northern spin to the group as well as specialist experience of fitting sustainability and local economic development into urban regeneration. So do the final members of the panel, Leeds' own John Thorp and, in the early days, the then head of urban renaissance at the regional development agency Yorkshire Forward, Alan Simpson. As this work progressed, it was Koetter Kim and John Thorp who drew it to a conclusion.

Simpson meanwhile set the sights of the new group to a suitably ambitious level on their first public outing. He told a launch party in Leeds that the city should resolve to be the Yorkshire Milan. Like Leeds, the Italian city has an illustrious industrial past and a heritage of fine buildings. 'It is seriously possible for us to emulate Milan as a 21st century galleried city, building on the wonderful history of our central area arcades', Simpson said. Initial thinking on such lines includes expanding the glassed-over network round the Victoria Quarter towards the Headrow, the Town and Civic Halls and Quarry Hill, and then – pace the aims of Vision 2 – to use urban-design excellence to make connections outwards from the city centre to the suburbs. Appropriately, these proposals would include the new City Museum at the former Civic Theatre where Lord Rogers, then head of the Urban Task Force, outlined the principles on which Renaissance Yorkshire was to be based in a lecture in 2001.

At the heart of this programme was the concept of the living city, a bustle of home life, work and enjoyment which Leeds has done remarkable things to achieve in the last 30 years. Progress continues towards a multi-purpose arena and the biggest programme of public art and green landscaping the city has seen, symbolised by a new initiative at the much-loved and recently refurbished Town Hall. When crowds filled the building for the premiere of 'The March of the Rhinos', Carl Davis' anthem to Leeds international rugby league champions, high above them in the clock and bell chamber electronic gear installed by the Californian sound artist Bill Fontana was going to work. His system zips digital recordings to the entrance of the neighbouring Art Gallery, filling the space around Rodin's *Age of Bronze* with ticks and tocks. On the hour, every hour, the first chime from the Town Hall clock reaches the ears of people in the gallery just before the actual clang of the bell arrives at the speed of sound – a delightful game with time. 'Come to Leeds and walk into the future', is Mr Fontana's motto. It could equally be the city's as it moves towards 2020.

207

LEEDS: A DIVERSE CITY

I arrived in Leeds from rural Cheshire as a small child, was educated and have spent my whole working life in Leeds. I feel very privileged to have a role in helping shape the present and future of this great City.

Leeds has, during my working lifetime, transformed itself from a post-industrial provincial city to one of the most economically successful and vibrant cities in England. Much of the city's resilience in periods of industrial decline and, more particularly, its reinvention in recent years is due to the diversity of the city and its people.

Leeds is almost unique among major UK cities, in that not only is it a major urban area, it also has a massive rural interland within its boundaries. Two thirds of the city is green with greenbelt agricultural land, its wonderful city parks and stately home estates. At the same time the quality of the built environment is very high on our agenda with major investments in our infrastructure, whether that's public realm, or new schools and houses, or a new museum and theatres. Everything which makes Leeds a quality place to live.

Economically the city has, for the last two centuries, been very diverse. This diversity continues into the 21st Century with not only a strong legal, financial and business services sector, second only to London, but also continued strength in manufacturing and a growth in new industries, such as the health and media sectors.

Finally, and most importantly, is the diversity of our people. The City has, for more than a century, welcomed people from around the world and this is reflected in the success of our business and cultural world. This makes us the exciting city we are!

For the future we need to continue to build upon this sound base to develop a strong, sustainable city, with real resilience to the vagaries of economic and climate change threats. I believe we can achieve this by protecting and enhancing the physical and economic diversity of the city; investing in the infrastructure and ensuring the built environment is of the highest quality and really addresses the climate change agenda; and that our investment in people ensures we have a skilled workforce who want to live and work in Leeds.

Our commitment to the quality of the built environment and investment in the infrastructure of the city remains a key component in demonstrating to the world we are a city of substance, depth and quality. My vision is that Leeds truly is one of the most prosperous, vibrant and attractive cities in Europe and that all the people of Leeds benefit from its prosperity.

JEAN DENT

Jean Dent is the Director of City Development at Leeds City Council which is one of the largest Local Authorities in the UK with a population of 750,000 people.

City Development brings together all the Council's physical, economic development, cultural and recreational activities, including asset management, design services, economic and business development, highways, libraries, arts and heritage, planning, recreation and sport.

Jean is a Fellow of the Royal Institution of Chartered Surveyors. She has spent all her working life at Leeds City Council and worked in many fields of property development, regeneration and economic development before being appointed Director of Development and now most recently Director of City Development.

She has played a very active role in the physical development and regeneration of the city working on a number of major schemes, which have helped transform the city. She is a member of RICS Regeneration Panel, the Steering Group of the Leeds Property Forum and is a Director of Marketing Leeds.

LEEDS

I have lived in Leeds for 35 years and loved it for as long. The changes have been immense, and mostly, if not all, to the good. So for my future vision I shall imagine Leeds at the end of another 35 years and I shall be idealistic but not entirely unrealistic. I shall try and concentrate on architecture, 'the poetry of construction', as Sir Thomas Jackson described it. However, I agree with Sir John Betjeman that 'architecture can not be defined. So many factors are concerned with it, the planning of towns, the increase of population, the conditions of life, the climate, the subsoil, the political tendencies of the people, their aesthetic desires…'; therefore my vision can range far.

But first, a word about process, which is of crucial importance if any worthwhile results are to be achieved. There must be networks of flexible and responsive partnerships which bring together all the energies and skills of a creative city. There must be room for talent to grow and learn and contribute and influence change. LADI was one example, 4 x 4 is another.

ROOFTOP LEEDS
The top of every building is worth looking down on
Every building is worth looking up at

OPEN SPACE LEEDS
Every town and village has a tree-shaded centre with comfy seat with backs
The children of every neighbourhood have their own spaces to play in

CONNECTED LEEDS
There are no barriers preventing pedestrians from taking the shortest, safest route
The ten new arcades and ten new ginnels extend the network of surprising choices

HIDDEN LEEDS
All footpaths are publicly registered, and in good order
Heritage Open Days are organised three times a year

CONTEXTUAL LEEDS
The arena is a gem of handsome architecture, nestling in its place and envied by every other city
Kirkstall Forge is all the best of Leeds in little

- Unemployment is no more than 2 per cent, the same in Wetherby as it is in Burmantofts.

- There are no glaring, blaring adverts whether on street lights or on hoardings.

- The A65 at Kirkstall Abbey has been tunnelled, and there is a continuous boulevard planted with 100 different kinds of tree from Horsforth to Wellington Street as there is along the A64 York Road.

- The Wellington Street flyover has gone and people know that to walk from the Town Hall to the Kirkstall viaduct is no further than from the Town Hall to the Royal Armouries.

- Traffic has gone from City Square.

- Children can go anywhere on their bikes.

- Our carbon footprint is neutral and there is no flooding.

- Every neighbourhood has its own design statement and vision of its own, CCUDS and Neighbourhoods for Living have been revised, all after intense public debate, and every developer abides by them.

- Leeds is recognised as the most intriguing, welcoming, attractive, lively, ambitious, artistic city and its citizens as the most kind, friendly, imaginative, open and caring, if also blunt and to the point.

- Turnout at local elections is 80 per cent.

- Leeds Rhinos are top of the League.

LIZ MINKIN

Elizabeth Minkin was elected as a Labour councillor to represent Kirkstall ward on Leeds City Council in May 1988, ten years after starting the Kirkstall Village Community Association.

Her 20 years on the Council was a stimulating, frustrating and rewarding time. She became Chair of the Planning Committee in 1992. The immensely steep learning curve made her realise the huge gaps in understanding among all involved, so she set up the Leeds Architecture and Design Initiative in 1994.

In 1999, she became the Executive Board member responsible for Planning, Transport, Tourism and Economic Development, until Labour lost control in 2004.

She was a CABE Festive Five Design Champion in 2002 and made an Honorary Fellow of RIBA in 2003. Elizabeth retired from Council in 2008, and was made Honorary Alderman of Leeds.

A SPATIAL PLANNER'S VISION FOR THE CITY REGION

Having experienced work at Leeds City Council Planning Department at the tender age of 16, I have always had a great admiration and respect for the work of our Planners, Architects and Engineers in shaping my home city of Leeds into one of the best places to live in the UK. Indeed, it was this experience of working with Leeds City Council Planning Officers as a school boy from Moortown, north Leeds, which encouraged me to take up town and country planning as a career and shape successful places for people in which to live, work and play to the fullest.

This Spatial Planner's Future Vision for the City of Leeds is a peace-loving cosmopolitan place which is outward looking as well as inward looking. It will play a pivotal part of the Great Northern Trans Pennine Metropolis stretching from Liverpool to Hull and will truly be at the heart of the Leeds City Region. Leeds City Council officers, politicians and partners will work collaboratively with their counterparts in the Districts of Bradford, Barnsley, Calderdale, Craven, Harrogate, Kirklees, Selby, Wakefield, York and North Yorkshire County Council with the sole aim of fulfilling the vision, which in the words of our 11 City Region Partners (Leeds City Region Development Programme 2006) is:

'To develop an internationally recognised city-region; to raise our economic performance; to spread prosperity across the whole city region; and to promote better quality of life for all of those that live and work here.'

The Leeds City Region at the heart of the Great Northern Trans Pennine Metropolis will truly rival the world city of London in terms of sheer size, economic clout and its second-to-none retail and leisure offer. The city will welcome large numbers of people northwards from the south to take up new home grown job opportunities in the financial, business, creative and knowledge industries and experience the high quality of life already enjoyed for decades by the people of Leeds. The city will have excellent transport infrastructure with high speed Trans Pennine train routes and high speed lines between Scotland, London and Europe with their 200 mph magnetic levitation trains.

The future will see new Ebenezer Howard Garden City-inspired urban extensions to Leeds, with zero carbon two-storey semi-detached houses, front and back gardens, local neighbourhood shopping parades, new parklands and world class education and health care provision. All this supported by a combination of high quality tram, train and hydrogen fuel powered bus links which will plug the new garden city extensions into the existing city regional network. The character of established and new Leeds suburbs will be protected from high density developments, which have been such a prominent feature of central and inner parts of Leeds. The suburbs of Leeds will continue, as they always have done, to fulfil people's housing aspirations, with greater protection of historic buildings, spaces, sports playing fields, allotments and green open spaces for future generations to enjoy.

This is my future vision.

BHUPINDER DEV

Bhupinder Dev, MRTPI, Senior Planning Officer at Bradford City Council. Leeds born and bred, Bhupinder studied Town Planning at the University of Manchester and Urban Design at Leeds Metropolitan University. He has experience of working on regeneration projects in Leeds, such as the Leeds Bradford Corridor Study, Garnetts Paper Mill, Otley, Leeds Waterfront Strategy Review and the Aire Valley Hunslet Stourton Environmental Improvement Plan through previous employment with White Young Green and Gillespies.

A member of the RTPI Yorkshire Committee, Director of Concourse (Leeds Architecture Centre) and the founder of YORnet (the network for young built environment professionals in Yorkshire). He actively works with RIBA and RTPI in organising interdisciplinary seminars and networking events for planners, architects and engineers in the city. Bhupinder is also a member of Roundhay Planning Forum and enjoys working with fellow residents on the Neighbourhood Design Statement for the historic Leeds suburb of Roundhay.

LEEDS AS A CITY REGION: ARCHITECTURE MEETS GEOGRAPHY

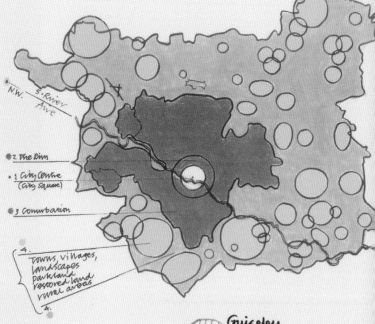

During the period of the shaping of this book, Simon Jenkins' observation that Leeds 'understands its urbanity' was, for me, a constant point of reference.

It seems that the architecture of its streets, spaces and arcades matters as much to Leeds as does the architecture of individual buildings – magnificent as many are.

The structure of the city is there to be found in the remarkable survival of patterns of development from all key historical phases of the evolution of the city.

My first hope is that this gradualist, subtle art of shaping place will continue to be understood and patiently practised.

A second hope for the future is that the rich diversity of landscapes and architectural detail which covers the 220 square miles of the contemporary city of Leeds will continue to be celebrated and enriched.

I believe that this extensive 'geographical city' set amongst its equally diverse but complementary neighbours - contains the potential to connect experiences of urban, suburban and rural conditions into a coherent city landscape. This exceptionally diverse character might also enable Leeds to make the transition from a post-industrial condition into a new ecologically sustainable city.

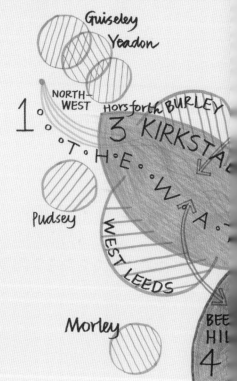

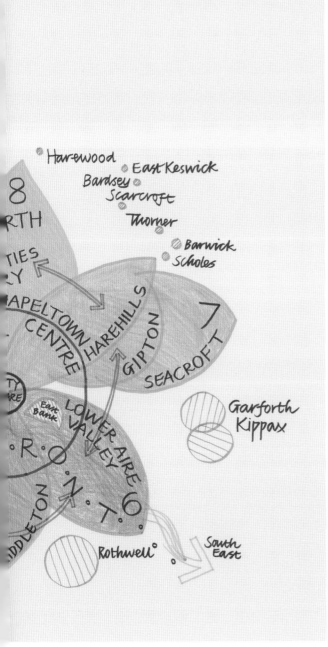

JOHN THORP

John Thorp has been Civic Architect for Leeds City Council since 1996 – a role which includes the creation and delivery of an urban renaissance for the city and the enabling of high quality design.

John has worked for the city in several architectural roles for 38 years.

He is a member of the 2012 CABE / DfL Olympic Games Design Review Panel and of the CABE Olympic Legacy Design Review Panel. He was a member of the national CABE Design Review Panel for 5 years. He is also a CABE 'Inspirer' for schools.

John is a member of the Leeds Architecture and Design Initiative and 'Concourse' (Architecture Centres Network) - bodies which champion and promote inter-sector and inter-disciplinary working in art, architecture, landscape and public space.

John was awarded the M.B.E. for services to architecture in the Queen's New Year's Honours list, 2005.

THE FOUNDATIONS ARE CAST

The City of Leeds has experienced dramatic and transformational change over the last twenty years. Being born, educated and working in Leeds, I am bound to have a deep passion for the city – but particularly for ensuring that Change is not just for change's sake but that it can make a real and positive difference to people's lives. Growth and prosperity is important – but growth and prosperity through investment in quality places and spaces is even more so.

When I founded Rushbond, back in the mid 1980s, the city was a much different place in which to do business. Looking back, the sheer scale of change has actually been quite remarkable. What has been important over this time is that the commitment to quality place making has been a shared commitment by all that have helped shape the city's transformation.

The citizens of Leeds are proud of their city and its heritage – I certainly am. Making sure we keep in touch with the past, and what made this city great, is vitally important as the city progresses and changes. I hope that we never lose it.

The challenges that are faced in delivering real change can only be tackled, and successful projects delivered, through working together in partnership – a much and perhaps over used word at times, but a word that signifies the only way of achieving sustainable growth of quality. There is a strong tradition of the public, private and voluntary sectors working with each other in Leeds. I hope that it will continue.

I would like to think that the commitment to quality has made sound business sense for those who have been prepared to take up the challenge. Investment in good design not only adds value to the city – it adds value to the bottom line, ensuring sustainable investment in its broadest sense. I hope that more continue to recognise this.

My Vision would see a city that continues to raise its game and is prepared to reject the average. A city that is not frightened by innovation but doesn't forget its legacy. A city that provides the support for those prepared to take up the challenge on delivering to a quality agenda. A city that has a reputation for getting things done.

The foundations are cast – the commitment to quality, the passion for new architecture and public art, the tradition of working in partnership, a sense of civic pride, a vibrant and diverse economy, and some great places and spaces. My vision is to ensure that we build upon these foundations. That in particular we set a clear agenda for real change in the communities that skirt the city centre – so that they become fully inclusive and truly benefit from the economic powerhouse that is the city centre. That we move into the future with a greater sense of shared confidence over what can be achieved. And to push the boundaries of what is achievable.

JONATHAN MAUD

Jonathan Maud is the founder and Managing Director of Rushbond plc.

Having been born and educated in the city, Leeds was a natural place for Jonathan to start a business. In the course of his career, he has produced some of the most innovative and interesting development projects in the city; from historic building conversions through to major mixed use schemes. These projects range from the restoration of Civic Court, Elmete Hall and Burley Mills to major new pieces of townscape through Brewery Wharf, on the city's waterfront, BBC Regional Headquarters at St Peters Square and Echo, a residential-led community along the city's eastern fringe, and reflected in numerous regional and national awards.

His particular passions include supportive and charitable works within Leeds and its disparate communities. This, along with a real belief in the value of art within the built environment and a hands-on style, remains an essential aspect to his work.

A CALL FOR CLARITY AND BOLDNESS OF PURPOSE

I love the grittiness of Leeds city centre with the intriguing glimpses of its great Georgian trading past, its wonderfully robust and yet ornate Victorian and Edwardian buildings, and the warmth and down-to-earth quality of its people seen at their best in the Aladdin's Cave which is Kirkgate Market. Yet still more fascinating are its suburbs and out-townships, above all Headingley and the Meanwood Valley where wandering through old stone-walled ginnels you may chance upon time-aged villa and terrace enclaves, close to meandering woodland and parkland becks. Here the regimentation of modern life is defied by the eccentricities of shanty town allotments with their hens and horses. The city's unique character, defined by the co-existence of the highly urban with the semi-rural, owes much to its radial green corridors running quickly into the countryside, its beautiful suburban parks and its rapidly disappearing large villa gardens and informal green spaces.

If this unique character is to be conserved amidst the growth of an attractive, prosperous city, Leeds City Council must have the confidence to abandon its short-term, 'incremental approach' to planning. Instead the city's development must be guided by a truly visionary and detailed spatial masterplan. The plan or suite of plans must anticipate the parameters of the world in which we will be living in the future and provide for a good mode of human living which can be sustained in the long term.

THE CITY CENTRE IN 2028

- The waterfront corridor will be the recreational heart of the city centre and the focus of new green space and major public amenities. Bridge End will be its vibrant hub linked to the shopping area by a revitalised Lower Briggate.

- The public realm of the largely pedestrianised city centre will be admired for its trees, grass, pocket parks, public art, and facilities for children. City Square and the Civic Quarter will be traffic free.

- The regenerated inner city rim will have been reintegrated with the city centre and the city centre will have been extended south of the river in fine-grained mixed-use development.

CITY WIDE IN 2028

- Today's out-of-town shopping centres will have closed and shopping, amenities and services will have been consolidated in the city's District Centres. The result will have been the renaissance of Morley, and an assured future for Otley and similar towns.

- People will move easily around the city on its convenient, safe, easily understood, and reliable fully integrated public transport system with Supertram at its core.

- Devolved decision-making and resources will have returned control of their local environment to the residents of the out-townships and satellite towns.

- This 'devolution', and meaningful consultation, will have ended the urban cramming and inappropriate infill development which today is gradually degrading the character of the city's suburbs. The city's increased population will have been housed in the southern extension of the city centre, along Kirkstall Road, and in the regenerated areas of Holbeck, Beeston and the Lower Aire Valley.

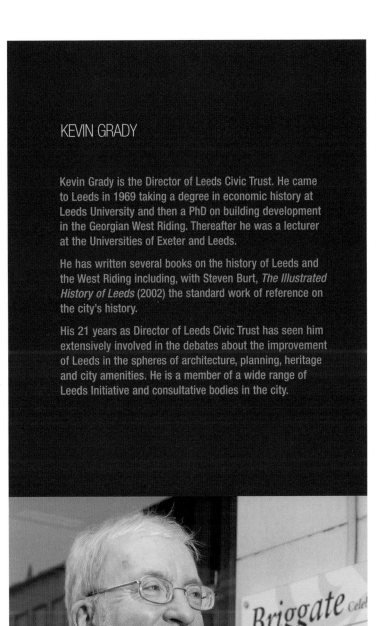

KEVIN GRADY

Kevin Grady is the Director of Leeds Civic Trust. He came to Leeds in 1969 taking a degree in economic history at Leeds University and then a PhD on building development in the Georgian West Riding. Thereafter he was a lecturer at the Universities of Exeter and Leeds.

He has written several books on the history of Leeds and the West Riding including, with Steven Burt, *The Illustrated History of Leeds* (2002) the standard work of reference on the city's history.

His 21 years as Director of Leeds Civic Trust has seen him extensively involved in the debates about the improvement of Leeds in the spheres of architecture, planning, heritage and city amenities. He is a member of a wide range of Leeds Initiative and consultative bodies in the city.

> Fireworks over
> Kirkstall Abbey
> WWW.JH-JPHOTO.CO.UK

FURTHER READING
LEEDS: SHAPING THE CITY

Leeds has been well-served by its historians, from the earliest days of Ralph Thoresby whose *Ducatus Leodiensis; or the Topography of the ancient and populous Town and Parish of Leedes and parts adjacent in the West Riding of the County of York*, was published in 1715. A second edition was published by Dr. T. D. Whitaker in 1816. In modern times, anything bearing the imprint of Leeds Civic Trust or written by its director Dr Kevin Grady and his frequent collaborator Steven Burt, is thoroughly worthwhile and trustworthy as are the scholarly works of the late Professor Maurice Beresford. Particularly recommended for an overall picture are:

Broadhead, I *Leeds*, Smith Settle (Otley, 1979).

Burt, S and Grady, K *The Illustrated History of Leeds*, Breedon Books (Derby, 2002).

Fraser, D (ed.) *A History of Modern Leeds*, Manchester University Press (Manchester, 1980).

Unsworth, R. and Stillwell, J (eds.) *Twenty-First Century Leeds: Geographies of a Regional City*, Leeds University Press (2004). Sixteen Chapters about the Contemporary City; 160 maps, many photos.

Wrathmell, S *Leeds*, Pevsner Architectural Guides, Yale University Press (London 2005).

More idiosyncratic studies of Leeds include the following, which take rather a specialised or partial view but, in doing so, illuminate the character of the city as a whole:

Beresford, M *Walks Round Red Brick*, (Leeds University Press 1980) and *East End, West End*, Thoresby Society (Leeds 1988).

Betjeman. J, *Leeds - A City of Contrasts*, is included in his collection *First and Last Loves*, John Murray, (London 1969).

Haughton, G & Williams, C (Ed) *Corporate City?*, Avebury Publishing (Aldershot, 1996).

Linstrum, D. *West Yorkshire - Architects and Architecture*, Lund Humphries (London, 1978) and *Historic Architecture of Leeds*, Oriel Press (1969).

Nuttgens, P *Leeds – the back to front, inside out, upside down city*, Stile Books (1979).

Sidey, P *Hello Mrs Butterfield – the story of Radio Leeds*, Kestral Press (1994).

Thompson, B *Portrait of Leeds*, Robert Hale & Co, (London 1971).

Waterhouse, K *City Lights*, Hodder & Stoughton (1994).

Many further books, booklets and pamphlets are available from Leeds Civic Trust, 17-19 Wharf Street, LS2 7EQ www.leedscivictrust.org.uk and the Thoresby Society, Claremont, 23 Clarendon Road, Leeds LS2 9NZ. www.thoresby.org.uk

The city's excellent library service is complemented by the independent Leeds Library, 18 Commercial Street, Leeds LS1 6AL enquiries@leedslibrary.co.uk, one of the oldest in the country whose founders included Joseph Priestley.